HACKING DEFICIT THINKING

8 REFRAMES THAT WILL CHANGE THE WAY YOU THINK ABOUT STRENGTH-BASED PRACTICES AND EQUITY IN SCHOOLS

HACK Learning
S E R I E S

**BYRON MCCLURE
& KELSIE REED**

Hacking Deficit Thinking
© 2022 by Times 10 Publications
Highland Heights, OH 44143 USA
Website: 10publications.com

All web links in this book are correct as of the publication date but may have
become inactive or otherwise modified since that time.

Cover and Interior Design by Steven Plummer
Editing by Jennifer Zelinger Marshall
Copyediting by Jennifer Jas

Paperback ISBN: 978-1-956512-24-3
eBook ISBN: 978-1-956512-25-0
Hardcover ISBN: 978-1-956512-26-7

Library of Congress Cataloging-in-Publication Data is available for this title.

First Printing: October 2022

To all educators who strive to reduce deficit thinking so students and adults alike can live a life of flourishing and rise to their full potential.

TABLE OF CONTENTS

SECTION ONE:
HISTORY, SYSTEMS, AND DATA

SECTION TWO:
THINKING, BELIEVING, AND FLOURISHING

HISTORY, SYSTEMS, AND DATA

INTRODUCTION
About This Book

"**A**T-RISK."
"Low."
"Lazy."
"Unmotivated."
"Not smart."
"Apartment kids."
"Title I kids."
"We already know where he will end up after high school."
"Her parents don't care about her."
"Education is not part of their culture."
"If they don't address it at home, there's nothing we can do."
"They don't want to succeed."
"He's just mimicking the problem behaviors he sees at home."
"This school is not a good fit for him."

If you have ever worked in a school, you have likely heard some of these coded labels or phrases; perhaps you've even said them yourself. While often stated by well-intentioned and unassuming educators, these phrases sum up deficit thinking.

"Deficit thinking" has become a wildly popular term in education. But what does it mean, and what does it look like in schools? We asked educators to define it for us, and we came to the following shared definition:

Deficit thinking is a distorted lens, focused on student weaknesses, that blames students and their families for student difficulties rather than acknowledging the impact of our practices and broader structural inequities.

Let's break that down.

1. **A distorted lens.** Biases about student abilities color our worldview and warp our reality. They may be based on our upbringing, stereotypes we've encountered over time, or harmful generalizations we believe. This is the power of deficit thinking. The longer we operate from this distorted lens, the more data we find that confirms false beliefs, and the more we will fail our students.

2. **Focused on student weaknesses.** This emphasis on student weakness is especially present when working with minority groups and students from marginalized backgrounds. It's based in racism, classism, sexism, ableism, and eugenics. It targets those historically identified as "inferior" and "unwelcome" in schools.

3. **That blames students and their families for student difficulties.** Our educational system originally supported the idea that only White, middle-class, able-bodied males deserved an education. They considered any other qualities a "weakness." (You'll learn more about that later.) By not valuing the strengths of all individuals, the blame begins.

   "If my instruction benefits some students and not others, it has to be the students' fault, right?"

"If some students know how to behave in my class, but others don't, it has to be the parents' fault, right?"

4. **Rather than acknowledging the impact of our practices and broader structural inequities.** School buildings and our larger society constantly contribute to and reinforce systemic racism and otherisms that impact our interactions with students. Blaming the students takes the responsibility off us.

Because this lens places all fault on the student, we lower our expectations for them, either intentionally or subconsciously. If we have low expectations for students, we aren't motivated to provide them with enrichment. We successfully allow ourselves to believe that we can't do anything to contribute to better outcomes. Yet, students will always rise to the level of expectation we have set for them. If the expectation is low, they will only grow so much because they believe in our judgments.

Now that we understand how pervasive and harmful deficit thinking can be, you may ask what you can do to discard such a powerful ideology. Fortunately, many practices aid in dismantling deficit thinking. However, if we want to discard the deficit model, we will be uncomfortable.

We can no longer easily place blame.

We need to look at our practices from a critical lens and accept that we are the problem nine times out of ten—whether it be our inability to truly see our students or not taking the time to listen.

INTENDED AUDIENCE

This book is intended primarily for teachers, administrators, and school-based support staff such as school psychologists, counselors, and related service providers. It may also be helpful in teacher training programs or other graduate preparation courses that set the foundation for our future educators. If you work with students or plan to work with students, this book is for you. It is chock-full of helpful information and tools to hack deficit thinking.

HOW TO USE THIS BOOK

This book offers value in a few areas. We will help you understand where deficit thinking stems from and why it is such a powerful narrative. This is important because it's difficult to unlearn harmful patterns until we understand *why* we think the way we do. Also, dismantling deficit thinking depends on our ability to self-reflect and self-correct. After we understand why we think the way we do, we can understand how to change our behaviors.

Then we can change our thinking and behaviors to recognize and acknowledge strengths within our students, our schools, and ourselves—to better serve everyone.

As we gathered the content of this book, we relied on a set of interviews we conducted with educators, input we received from Google Forms, and questions posed on Twitter. While we also relied on best practices and frameworks that education researchers identify, we wanted to build upon the words that came directly from people like you.

Serving as 50 percent personal self-reflection and 50 percent actionable classroom and schoolwide practices, this book allows you to identify and address deficit thinking within yourself and your practices. Looking at both will help you to better serve your students.

We divided this book into two sections: Background and Application. The background hacks (Reframes) involve the themes of history (Reframe 1), systems (Reframe 2), and data (Reframe 3). You need to understand these concepts to use the rest of the book.

The application hacks involve the themes of thinking (Reframes 4 and 5), believing (Reframes 6 and 7), and flourishing (Reframe 8). Each of these hacks offers a different opportunity to disrupt deficit thinking.

This book is part of the Hack Learning Series, but we've customized the language in the series template. Instead of calling each chapter a "Hack," we're calling it a "Reframe" because we're viewing beliefs differently. The Problem has been replaced by The Belief, followed by The Reframe.

Next, we discuss What You Can Do Tomorrow to reframe that belief through a short, bulleted list of action items. After that, you'll find A Blueprint for Full Implementation, with detailed steps to implement this Reframe. Then in the Overcoming Pushback section, we discuss potential barriers you may face and how to navigate them. Finally, we will show the Hack in Action with specific examples that:

- Demonstrate how reflecting on deficit beliefs or practices can improve student outcomes

- Show you how to start student conversations or activities to disrupt deficit narratives

- Offer practical tips for when you observe harmful beliefs or practices in schools

What you put into this book will determine what you get out of it. Because deficit thinking is so pervasive, you must actively engage with this book to fully understand it.

WHAT YOU WON'T FIND IN THIS BOOK

We don't intend for this book to serve as a quick fix to dismantle deficit thinking. As you will read, we argue that deficit thinking intertwines with every facet of our educational systems. A quick fix doesn't exist. This book will also not provide feel-good activities. Much, if not most, of this book encourages deep personal reflection into how you personally operate from (and contribute to) a deficit-oriented system and set of beliefs. This reflection will help you begin to unlearn this narrative. You must allow yourself to experience contradicting evidence.

Throughout this book, we emphasize the importance of holding high expectations for our students in order to chip away at deficit thinking. However, you will not find specific examples of high expectations curricula here. We aren't experts on curriculum or instructional practices of teachers, but we will direct you to the many experts in these areas.

We also don't intend to blame anyone for engaging in deficit thinking. We hope this book will allow everyone to see that we are all deficit thinkers, whether we know it or not. The magic begins once we accept that we suffer from conditioned deficit thinking. The magic is in our reflection, reframing, and intentional behaviors.

This goes for any distorted belief or cognitive distortion—the first step is admitting we have a problem.

In this case, "we" is the educational system. The "problem" impacts millions of students every day. We don't say this lightly.

This book may make you uncomfortable at times. That is intentional. Deficit thinking has become so comfortable within our schools that any counterthought will evoke unfamiliar feelings. We challenge you to welcome these unfamiliar feelings with open arms.

We asked educators to share where they see deficit thinking showing up within the field of education. Here are three of the responses:

"It's *everywhere*, in teachers' perspective, in structural policies, behavior management practices, discipline practices, and problem-solving meetings. IEP and special education [are] rooted in deficitness."

— Dr. Cyndy Alvarez, school psychologist

"It shows up in lesson design and classroom management planning, including how students are assessed, classroom rigorous experience, and goal setting."

— Cory Cain, dean of instruction

"Deficit thinking is ingrained in educational systems and culture at all levels. It shows up in language ('low'— if I had a dollar for every time someone described a student as 'low,' I would be a millionaire) and in systems."

— Wendy Turner, teacher

WE CAN SHIFT TO WHAT'S STRONG
Unlearning Deficits

Despite any circumstance, with an encouraging teacher and purposeful support, every child can learn anything, maybe not in the same time or same space, but they can learn.

— PAMELA TUCKER, INSTRUCTIONAL COACH

THE BELIEF:
THE DEFICIT MODEL IS THE RIGHT MODEL

NO MATTER OUR role in education, we all have learned the wrong things. Our minds have misled us. We have it wrong.

Even worse, we have gotten it wrong for way too long. It's not our fault, and we can't blame any one person, group, or philosophy. The truth is that if you are a teacher, school administrator, paraprofessional, school psychologist, school counselor, nurse, or any professional within education, then you were conditioned— or, shall we say, trained—to pinpoint what's not working!

We're trained to identify what's wrong with people.

Most teacher prep and graduate training programs are

hyper-focused on training new teachers to identify the weaknesses in students, and it's been this way for decades.

We, the authors of this book, are both school psychologists by training. We have collectively practiced in the public school system for close to fifteen years—don't let our baby faces fool you. Our graduate school training informed our practice (shout-outs to Abilene Christian University, Indiana University of Pennsylvania, and Loyola University Chicago). We both can unequivocally say that we love the universities where we studied. The professors at these institutions helped mold and shape us into sound practitioners. They taught us to think critically, use data to make informed decisions, and advocate for children.

Because of this training, we both understand the significance of using our abilities to critically challenge systems and practices that might be harmful to children. That is why, upon deep reflection, we both realize that most graduate prep programs have deeply rooted deficiency ideals. As a result, many educators become practitioners skilled and equipped with tools designed to identify the absolute worst in students.

Let's discuss.

As school psychologists, we will use our field as an example. You can extend these examples across education prep programs. Every first-year school psychology grad student takes a cognitive and intellectual assessment course. It is the bread and butter of our profession. For the most part, a cognitive assessment course introduces school psych graduate students to issues and methods of intellectual assessments—commonly referred to as IQ tests. Luckily, some school psych grad students receive background information on the history and thought process of IQ tests. Nerd out with us for a minute on a short and egregious history of IQ tests.

Around the early 1900s, eugenicists wanted a simpler way to evaluate human intelligence. They believed in "racial improvement" and planned breeding. They thought they could eliminate individuals with "inferior" qualities or traits. How do you go about determining who has undesirable traits? What exactly *are* undesirable traits? For starters, scientists and psychologists at that time hyper-focused on intelligence. They spent most of their time researching and creating tests to determine inferior intelligence levels.

A professor at Stanford University, Lewis Terman, made a new test for eugenicists to use. It was cheap, fast, and thought to be easy to assess large quantities of people. Terman assessed children and teenagers, and he tried to test adults too. He had trouble finding enough adults to test, so he decided to treat anyone over fourteen as an adult. Here is where it gets interesting. All the kids he tested were White and born in the US. He didn't test any kids born outside of the US.

Why did he exclude them? Here is what he had to say about immigrants:

> "The tests have told the truth. These boys are ineducable beyond the merest rudiments of training. No amount of school instruction will ever make them intelligent voters or capable citizens—they represent the level of intelligence, which is very, very common among Spanish-Indian and Mexican families of the Southwest and also among Negroes. Their dullness seems to be racial or at least inherent in the family stocks from which they come."
> —The Measurement of Intelligence by Lewis Terman.
> Houghton Mifflin, 1916, p. 91.

Terman openly believed that certain groups of people were naturally inferior to the majority culture.

It gets worse. No, really, it gets a lot worse ...

Terman continued developing his assessments to evaluate even larger quantities of people over the next few years. His work seemed ideal for, let's say, testing people for inclusion in the army, which is exactly what Terman and his team did. They planned and designed these assessments to determine which men should be officers in the army and which men shouldn't be allowed in at all.

These tests were designed to include some and isolate others, a trend you will start to notice. But stay with us.

Between May and June of 1917, Terman and his crew refined these assessments and ultimately created several alpha and beta tests to determine whether men were unfit to serve. It's important to note what was happening in 1917. The United States entered World War I in April of 1917 as the country declared war on Germany.

That's a lot, but that's not all that happened during that time. This guy by the name of Robert Yerkes, the then-president of the American Psychological Association (yup, the same APA that recently put out an apology in 2021–2022 for their contribution to racism in America) formed a workgroup called the Committee on Methods of Psychological Examination for Recruits. This committee included Terman—the same guy who said that non-Whites are inherently dull because of their race.

The committee decided to focus on intelligence testing. The committee's goal was to *checks notes*: "Segregate and eliminate the mentally incompetent." Based on the committee's work, they ultimately tested and recommended close to eight thousand men be discharged due to "mental incompetence." Importantly, Terman thought intelligence was "fixed" and genetically determined. (We'll talk more about fixed mindsets later.)

So, what happened? We kid you not—Terman, a Stanford professor (who believed intelligence was racially and genetically determined), went on to collaborate with a man named Alfred Binet.

You might wonder, "Who is Alfred Binet?"

Well, at that time, Binet was widely known in France for developing a cognitive scale made popular for measuring children's intelligence. Terman and Binet collaborated to refine an intellectual ability test. This test, a product of Binet and Terman, again—a professor at Stanford—became known as the Stanford-Binet.

Here's the kicker: universities still train school psychologists to use the Stanford-Binet today.

The big question is, knowing this history of cognitive assessments, why do school psychologists use this tool? They receive training to administer tools that were created to evaluate deficits. Even worse, these tools identify deficits steeped in radical ideologies—based on eugenics.

Remember, segregating and eliminating those deemed mentally incompetent were aims of the Committee on Methods of Psychological Examination

> **School leaders, teachers, and every other practitioner within the field of education receive training to view students from a lens of identifying weaknesses and deficits.**

for Recruits. The American Psychological Association president spearheaded it at that time. It didn't stop there, either, and it's not only in the field of school psychology. These types of practices and training extend across the education landscape. For example, after the war ended, a Princeton professor, Carl Brigham, supported the Army Alpha test so much that he developed his own test. You might have heard of it.

It's called the Scholastic Achievement Test, commonly referred to as the SAT.

School psychology graduate students trained within this deficit model become school psychology practitioners. Then they become school psychology practitioners trained to identify deficits and weaknesses—for the purpose of labeling people.

Perhaps this is why school psychologists are referred to as "the gatekeepers of special education."

What does this currently look like inside of schools? These assessments sort kids into general education or special education. Guess which kids are often placed within special education? Our historically marginalized and minoritized kids. You'll learn more about this in later Reframes. The key point here is that most school psychologists practice a deficit model. The process of identifying what's wrong with people and what skills they might lack, and finding ways to solve problems, is baked into the very fabric of our field.

Importantly, the deficit model doesn't only apply to school psychologists. In this book, we argue that school leaders, teachers, and every other practitioner within the field of education receive training to view students from a lens of identifying weaknesses and deficits.

In this book, we push your thinking. Shifting away from a deficit lens requires real work. It will be hard work—but it will be worth it. By the time you finish reading this book, we hope you will be on fire to unlearn deficit thinking—and encourage others to put in the work to shift from **what's wrong (a deficit-based approach) to what's strong (a strength-based approach)**.

The most pressing question we must ask is this: Why do we (educators as a collective, despite your position) continue to use practices rooted within a deficit model? We argue that it's because of an inherent belief stemming from education training and practice. It taught us that the deficit model is the right model.

Let's look at an interview with Dr. Brandon Gamble, a school psychologist and the director of San Diego State University's Black Resource Center, as he sheds more light on this deficit thinking approach.

"We have to highlight what's right with people."
— Dr. Brandon Gamble

We asked Dr. Gamble for his take on deficit thinking. He begins by sharing a practice that educators and school psychologists alike must stop doing *immediately*: labeling people.

> "Stop just labeling people with numbers, but look at what it takes for them to learn what they need to learn. And this is a very different way of practicing psychology. I'm practicing, maybe more what some people might call community psychology. I'm doing a bit of social psychology, but I'd like to call it just soul work, right? Psych is the study of the soul, not just study of, but actual practice, right? As school psychologists, we should be particularly concerned with our practices. We shouldn't just be talking about it. We shouldn't just be measuring and labeling people. We should provide them with how to overcome their challenges.
>
> So that's what we should be assessing, the capacity of a young person. If a child comes to us who is struggling, as educators, we must be asking, "What can we do to help solve that particular problem?"

Remember how, earlier in this Reframe, we spoke about intelligence testing? Dr. Gamble practices in California, where an interesting event happened. You see, the state of California ended up prohibiting IQ assessments for African American children. Here's a brief history.

In 1971, the San Francisco Unified School District placed five African American children into special education classes for the "educable mentally retarded," also referred to and abbreviated as

EMR. (We now refer to this as an intellectual disability.) Their families filed suit in the Federal District Court of Northern California, claiming the students were wrongly placed in the classes. They based this claim on the students' performance on racially biased and discriminatory intelligence tests.

The complaint further alleged that a disproportionately large number of Black students were placed in EMR classes when compared with the total number of Black students in the school system, meaning that it's much more likely Black students would be placed in those programs compared to White students when you consider the number of students who were Black versus White.

The court sided with the students and forced the district to discontinue using IQ tests to place African American students in EMR classes.

It was only right we asked Dr. Gamble about this infamous Supreme Court case, and here's what he had to say:

"One of those students [involved in the Supreme Court case] is named Darryl Lester, and he's still alive and well, living in the Washington area. But before that, he lived in the San Francisco area, and they did not assess him well, nor did they follow up and help him with his actual problem. His actual problem was learning how to read. No one had taught him how to read. So, their limited assessment, their assessment was only limited to him sitting down and someone flipping pages and then coming up with the test score and saying, all right, let's call it a day—you are educably mentally retarded.

"But here's how the conversation would go present-day in the teacher's lounge: 'You know, he's very low.' But no one would have asked some crucial questions.

Did they ever actually *teach* this child how to read? Let's say if it comes to students with difficulties with math, then did they ever actually teach them how to do math?

"So, Black children and all children going from first grade to third grade, they're learning to read. But the hump is in third grade to fourth grade. They start reading to learn, and if they don't make it past that, they're going to struggle the rest of their time in school, so at some point, they need to be able to read to learn. So, if we're reviewing a child for a learning disability to see if those other pieces are happening, we have to ask questions about the instruction.

"When you start asking questions about the instruction, you're asking teachers very personal questions, or you're asking administrators very personal questions about their career, and it's not really personal. It's kind of professional, right? Did you teach this child how to read? Oh, apparently you didn't 'cause here they are. Now, this poses a challenge—do we blame the child? Or at least say that the problem resides within the child? Do we say that the problem is outside the child? Or do we find some balance of both? I don't even like to go with the first two. I just assume that there's some balance of both, and we need to tighten up both going forward."

Dr. Gamble called out another issue, particularly with the Larry P. court case and the other families represented.

"The courts found that the system was training school counselors and sometimes teachers or speech and language pathologists to give a single test, and that was it. Then, school teams would make their determination and make placements based on that, which was creating what we called the 'six-hour retarded job.' So, they're retarded for six hours at school, but they go home, they're making change for their mother at the store. They're going to church, memorizing large verses of scripture songs, they're playing in the band. They're preaching. There's a range of behaviors that they're engaging in.

"You're like, hmm. Are they actually what these test scores say they are, or is it that the test score being the only indicator is the problem? Another concern was that parents of these students were never interviewed, and I still see that to this day. But what I'm talking about is being willing to hear their voice and incorporate a more complete picture of the child into your conversations, into your hypothesis-driven assessment. Again, it goes back to how we were trained."

We asked Dr. Gamble to share a little more about the thinking that underlies a deficit model.

"The thinking generally is, 'Okay. There's something wrong. If we could find out what's wrong, then maybe we can help remediate that.' I would say that if we're looking for optimal functioning, then we're going to build on the optimal functioning. ... As Dr. Asa Hilliard said, we must believe that all children are geniuses. They have something special that they do that they brought to the world, so we have to highlight that. So, we counter some of that deficit model thinking to begin to high-light what's right with people."

THE REFRAME:
WE CAN SHIFT TO WHAT'S STRONG

Have you ever felt that your training did not match how you should practice teaching? Do you instinctively believe that young people can thrive when given the right tools and strategies and optimal conditions (or even despite adverse conditions)? We optimistically believe that most teachers see the potential of young people, and it's why many of us decided to become educators in the first place. We deeply believe that everyone has a unique strength that we should cultivate and tap into. But what we see day to day as practitioners typically and unfortunately runs against our beliefs.

To us, it's simple and goes back to what Dr. Hilliard said—all children are geniuses with something special to offer. When you operate from the belief that students have potential, you intentionally decide to say that every student can succeed. It is the job of educators to recognize that potential and draw from it so students might thrive. Again, it's not easy; it can and will frustrate you at times.

By shifting away from a deficit model, you choose to see the best in people, and then magic can happen. But how do you shift away from it? Logically, you must shift toward something else. We put forth shifting toward a strength-based approach.

A strength-based approach helps people learn to use their strong points, skills, talents, and abilities to face challenges, resolve conflicts, design innovative solutions, and change the world. It focuses on developing a person's unique strengths. For students, it's a model that promotes academic achievement, happiness, a sense of self-efficacy, and gratitude.

A strength-based approach concentrates on the positive attributes of a person or a group rather than on the negative ones. It is used in therapy, social work, leadership, and more to help individuals build their strength. It views people as resourceful, resilient, and more than any adverse condition they might encounter.

This approach is highly dependent on the individual's thought process and emotional information processing. It allows for open communication and thought processes so individuals can identify their value and assemble their strengths and capacities in the course of change.

A strength-based approach examines the individual and the person's environment. For example, it looks at systems operations, especially unbalanced power between a system or service and the people it is supposed to serve.

In a strength-based approach, the focus is on developing a student's unique strengths with a more positive outlook. It views students as resourceful and resilient. It doesn't just tell students what they're doing wrong; it empowers them to learn from their mistakes.

This approach is a useful way to encourage students with learning difficulties without making them feel defeated or inadequate.

If you're like most educators, you spend a lot of time identifying your students' weaknesses and trying to fix them. That's understandable and, at times, necessary—but it can also be disheartening to a young person. Alternatively, a strength-based approach focuses on students' strengths, talents, and abilities and aims to help them find activities they enjoy while leveraging their strengths they can focus on. There are many ways to do this, and educators can work together toward the same goal: helping each student find their unique strengths and passions.

A strength-based approach in the classroom might include the following:

- Discussing positive traits. For example, if you notice that one student loves art class, you might discuss how she could share her love of art with the other students via conversation or project ideas.

- Holding routine strength-based discussions. This lets your students know that their strengths matter to you.

- Helping students build skills to last a lifetime. You'll shift your thinking and understand that students are resourceful and resilient, and you can help them build on their strengths.

Practice applying this approach to your life in addition to applying it to your work with students. Find what you're good at and what you enjoy doing, and use those activities to be the best version of yourself. To find what you are good at, begin by naming your strengths. Once you can name your strengths, you can begin to understand each one. Once you understand your strengths, then you can apply them to your daily life. We will discuss this more shortly.

A strength-based approach is unique because it centers on the needs of people from a lens that is optimistic, value-centered, innovative, resilient, and collaborative. Put people first.

A key element of a strength-based approach is setting and achieving goals, which helps to create change. Setting goals will help you move from one state of being to another—from where you are now to where you want to be. When setting goals, think about how you want to feel while achieving them. If your goal is too difficult, you may become discouraged or distressed by your perceived failure. If your goal is too easy, you may become complacent or bored and not challenged enough. Aim to set goals that align with what you want for yourself and your life.

Remember that social support, capital, and resources matter! In a strength-based approach, students recognize their strengths and the strengths of others, and they learn how to leverage the strengths of other people. For example, a student might be strong with historical facts but need help with complex math equations. They may have a friend who is strong with math equations and agrees to help them study for the math test in exchange for helping them with an upcoming history quiz. In this example, both students use the social capital they've built with each other while simultaneously leveraging their strengths. To sum it up, Charlamagne Tha God put it best: "Relationships and manners can take you where money can't."

To begin unlearning the deficit model and deficit thinking, you start with a strength-based approach. Instead of identifying the worst in people, you shift to looking for what's right with people.

WHAT YOU CAN DO TOMORROW

We need to shift away from the deficit model and focus on what is right with people. To do so, we must first understand their needs by adopting a human-centered approach, meaning putting people first.

- **Understand the meaning of a human-centered approach.** Schools trained and conditioned educators to identify problems using a deficit lens and a deficit approach to working with students. This type of approach prioritizes what is wrong, focuses on weaknesses, and aims to eradicate problems. We are not saying to ignore weaknesses and only focus on strengths, because this can present a different set of problems. Rather, we are suggesting you find ways to leverage the strengths of people by building up student skills in a thoughtful and meaningful way. Adopt a human-centered approach that focuses on developing solutions to problems by prioritizing the needs of people.

- **Add more empathy to your day.** In this context, empathy runs deeper than just putting yourself in the shoes of others. Within a human-centered approach, empathy requires us to understand people's thoughts, feelings, passions, and unmet needs on a deeply intimate level. A practical way to add empathy to your day is talking with people. You can ask a colleague to have coffee or lunch as a way to listen to their needs. You can have a weekly lunch bunch with a small group of students as a simple but meaningful way to understand their thoughts and feelings. The key here is to take the time to create a space where you can listen deeply to the needs of others. See Image 1.1 for examples of the types of questions you may want to ask.

Ask clarifying questions:
- Who am I seeking to understand and learn more about?
- What matters to this person?

Ask neutral questions:
- What do you think about _____?

Ask questions that explore emotions:
- Why do you feel _____?
- What do you feel about _____?

Ask why:

To dig deeper into understanding emotions and what motivates people, ask "why."
- Why?
- Why do you think that _____?
- Why do you _____?

Image 1.1: Types of questions.

- **Ask the right questions.** Another way to dig deeper into understanding people's thinking, actions, and behaviors is to ask good follow-up questions. After you ask a question and realize you need more information, say, "Can you tell me a little more about that?" Boom! This gently pushes people to further explore and shed more insight that can help you understand what they might be thinking or experiencing. You might also ask, "What were you feeling at that moment?" This is another great question because it helps you see and learn more about how they felt and how it impacted them.

A BLUEPRINT FOR FULL IMPLEMENTATION

The key to a human-centered mindset lies in focusing on people's needs and authentically listening to them. It's looking for inspiration and seeking solutions. To shift your mindset, practice these seven steps to human-centered design and note how they differ from your approaches to life right now.

Step 1: Embrace empathy.

For too long, educators, scholars, and researchers have attempted to solve problems in education without truly empathizing with and understanding the people they serve. We need to sincerely and authentically empathize with people to capture the complexity of the situations we encounter. Empathy helps us solve problems and enhance creative solutions. How often do you take the needs of everyone involved into consideration? Aim to be more intentional about considering everyone.

Step 2: Seek optimism.

To be clear, we are not suggesting you ignore problems. That causes more harm than good. Instead, make it a habit to practice a healthy sense of optimism in your work—the belief that positive outcomes are possible and that you can find solutions. As educators, we must believe that progress can solve our problems.

Step 3: Practice iteration.

We must perpetually improve and refine our work to create better solutions. Iterating allows us to develop ideas quickly and repeatedly test our ideas to see what's working and what's not. We learn from our mistakes, and our solutions become more effective.

Step 4: Find your creative confidence.

Acknowledge that you have creative ideas. Creative confidence allows educators to trust their instincts about real solutions to problems. You know your stuff, but sometimes, impostor syndrome, self-doubt, and a deficit mindset block and diminish your self-assurance. You must intentionally permit yourself to be confident. Once you build it and own it, you can channel your confidence into creativity.

Create things, test them out, make mistakes, and keep on creating as you develop skills and habits. Your creative confidence grows as you achieve small successes and then build to bigger achievements.

Step 5: Make it.

How often have you, a colleague, or someone you know just admired a problem? What did that do? The answer is nothing. For some reason, in the space of education, we became experts in admiring problems—which benefits no one. Instead, express your idea for a solution and take steps to implement it. If the problem involves students, for example, you might consider creating a student needs survey to better understand their desires. Write down questions you can ask students and then create a short Google survey. You can also get feedback from staff to further refine the survey. Then consider the feedback and move forward with implementing your solution.

Step 6: Embrace ambiguity.

Sometimes, we have no clue what is going on—or even what the problem is. When we can't define or understand a problem, we can't imagine a solution. While it may feel uncomfortable, we can open ourselves up to new ideas and arrive at an unexpected solution by embracing ambiguity, which means we leave it open to more than one possibility. We might have preconceived notions (this goes back to the deficit thinking approach) of why something won't work. We might hear, "That kid can't learn," or "I had their sibling, and the apple doesn't fall far from the tree." These types of preconceived notions limit our ability to creatively and confidently solve problems. Educators can reach creative ideas and look at problems from an unexpected perspective by thinking about all possibilities for innovative solutions.

Step 7: Learn from failure.

Use failure as a tool to improve your practices. A human-centered design mindset begins with not knowing the solution to a challenge, and that's okay. What's not okay is doing nothing.

How often have we had the world's best idea or even a small idea, but we never knew what could have been because we let our fear paralyze us—and instead, we did nothing? Let's use every opportunity to experiment and grow from our mistakes, reframing them as opportunities to improve and try something new.

Failure is a part of life—and especially a part of education. When things go wrong, as they sometimes will, we must ask, "What is the learning opportunity here?" We can intentionally take advantage of these opportunities rather than shying away from them, and we will grow and move toward innovative solutions. The key takeaway: we can't solve problems if we don't try something better.

OVERCOMING PUSHBACK

Most of us have been conditioned as educators to believe that the deficit model is the right model. We are experts in identifying the worst in people. Because of this belief, it can be challenging to believe anything to the contrary. When shifting from a deficit-based approach to a human-centered approach that leverages people's strengths, you will inevitably encounter pushback.

Some students just don't have any strengths. Like Dr. Hilliard said—all children are geniuses. It is up to us to discover and unlock that genius. Know that we are not here to be saviors or to operate under the belief that it is us and only us who can "help kids." Instead, we must believe that all children are geniuses and approach our work with the attitude that we can help cultivate and unlock that raw genius in our children. We can, and we must, create the right conditions inside of our schools where children feel safe and supported to show their genius.

This is the way I've always done it. Just because that's the way you've always done it doesn't mean it's the right way or the most effective way. It also doesn't mean it's the most meaningful or impactful way. When you dig deeper and push the thinking of those who say things like "I've always done it that way," or "Things will never change because it's always been done like that," you will find out that they don't know why they do things in a certain way. Hopefully, they will come to realize that the comfort of familiarity is not as valuable as the benefits of changing to a better way.

I need to focus on evaluation. The field of education and many graduate training programs are rooted in identifying what's wrong with people. Educators, clinicians, and school leaders are masterfully skilled at pinpointing weaknesses in students and even in each other. Just because education is inherently grounded in a deficit approach based on evaluation doesn't mean it is the right approach. The good news is that we don't have to believe in a deficit ideology. This starts with noticing and reflecting on your beliefs and how they show up in your practices. It involves accepting alternative approaches such as human-centered or positive psychology. It's okay to have creative confidence and believe that every kid is a genius. Put in relentless work to create the conditions where young people can thrive within their zone of genius.

THE REFRAME IN ACTION

Ms. Stanton has a large poster behind her desk that says: "Everybody is a genius. But if you judge a fish by its ability to climb a tree, it will live its whole life believing that it is stupid."

She has taught students receiving special education services for more than twenty-five years. Since she first began teaching, she has believed in the limitless potential of her students.

As an educator, Ms. Stanton explains how she has seen initiatives come and go. She has seen staff turnover along with new administration and school leaders. She recalls learning about new policies and seeing them fizzle out, and experiencing her fair share of grants and initiatives: some were successful, and some were not.

Despite the changes, trends, turnover, and ever-evolving education landscape, Ms. Stanton says that her approach to students has never changed. As a newly minted teacher, she vowed to view every student as a genius. She understood that each child has challenges, but she also knew each child had potential. She never accepts less than what she knows her students are capable of. She sets high expectations and does her best to help every student. She asks them, "How will you use your genius today?"

Ms. Stanton's approach to education is simple, and the poster behind her desk illustrates it perfectly. She believes so deeply that each child has a unique strength that she purposed her entire life to help children, every year, find their strengths and use them. She would have lunch with her students to get to know them, learn about their interests, and listen to their challenges. She routinely completed strength observations and then offered daily feedback to her students. One day, she worked with a new student named Jason who had recently transferred to the school. The school often placed new students in her class. Jason received special education services as a student with an emotional disability, and he struggled with math. During a math test, Jason grew increasingly frustrated. Several questions into the test, he had reached his limit and began to emotionally shut down. He couldn't handle failure. Ms. Stanton caught Jason in the midst of ripping up his paper.

She looked Jason firmly in the eyes and said, "Fail today, learn tomorrow, keep the lesson."

Jason was confused by her response and didn't know if he should keep ripping up the paper or finish the test. So, he sat for the remainder of the test.

After she dismissed the students, Jason went to Ms. Stanton and said, "I know I failed."

She replied, "Yes, you did, but you will learn tomorrow."

She explained that failure is okay, getting frustrated is okay, but to never miss the lesson. The lesson she was teaching Jason is that everyone, at some point, will experience failure, but it doesn't mean that you are a failure.

Jason replied, "You mean I'm not a failure?"

Ms. Stanton said, "Of course not; you failed the test, but Jason is not a failure."

She then praised him for being resilient and overcoming challenges. Ms. Stanton told Jason how she had been watching him and noticed that he could bounce back from difficult situations. He likely had rarely heard someone speak affirmatively to him because teachers had always labeled him as "a bad child." People told him for so long that he, as a person, was a failure, so he internalized it to his core. Jason internalized being a failure so deeply that he began to live up to those limiting beliefs other people had put on him. But Ms. Stanton permitted him to redress those beliefs. She allowed him to retake the test. The next time he took the test, he got two more items right than he did the first time he took it. He beamed with joy. He didn't exhibit frustration. He had put forth focus and effort, and he felt proud about finishing the test.

Jason said, "Ms. Stanton, I'm resilient, and I know I will bounce back next time because I'm not a failure. I just failed this test."

Some students may never have the good fortune of being educated by a teacher like Ms. Stanton. You can help to change this scenario. Since you've made it this far in this book, you are serious about doing the work of shifting from what's wrong to what's strong. We know you have what it takes to be a Ms. Stanton in the lives of the young people you work with.

We *can* stop deficit thinking. We *can* shift toward what's strong personally and professionally. As educators, we *can* believe that every kid is a genius. Ms. Stanton made it her mission to see the potential of every student who entered her classroom. She skillfully helped her students name their strengths and discover new ways to use them. If you want to shift toward what's strong, strive to be like Ms. Stanton—someone who sees the limitless potential in students. When you move away from deficit thinking, you say the problem isn't within children—it's within the system.

2

OUR PROBLEMS EXIST WITHIN THE SYSTEM
Fix Injustice Not Kids

The education system is so broken by White supremacy, patriarchy, and capitalism, so it's normal for educators to be frustrated or overwhelmed at times because our problems are big and systemic, and a lot of the time, we don't have the resources or authority to address them ... Deficit thinking sneaks in, and instead of naming systemic barriers, we name students or their families as the problem.

— SHANNON WILLIAMSON, DIRECTOR OF A LEARNING RESOURCE CENTER

THE BELIEF:
OUR PROBLEMS EXIST WITHIN THE CHILD

WE ASKED OUR social media followers to share common deficit thinking phrases they hear in their schools regarding students. Have you heard any of these comments?

"They're just REALLY low."

"They're just bad."

"They just don't care as much about education because it's not part of their culture."

"That kid is just lazy."

41

If you have spent any time inside of a school, you have probably heard similar comments. These comments are rooted in deficit thinking, which centers the blame on the child or their family, community, or culture. This belief falsely blames the student, and it's dangerous for several reasons. For starters, it assumes that a student's potential is fixed and the student can't grow or evolve. Also, it reinforces the idea that a child is inherently inferior. When people make comments like "That child can't learn" or "The apple doesn't fall far from the tree," it's coded language for "The child is intellectually, physically, or emotionally less than their peers." It's a way to attribute weaknesses and deficiencies that become part of who that child is, and no one can do anything about it. The danger in this line of thinking is that it doesn't allow room for growth, teaching, or learning. It sets the standard for low expectations.

The answer? Address the root cause of the problem, not the child. Examine the conditions that are perpetuating the poor outcomes. Students are people, not outcomes, not data points, and not statistics. If students aren't learning or growing as measured by outcomes, then you must examine what's happening from an ecological and systemic approach. Notice and reflect on how systemic inequities have led to injustices in certain communities across generations. Every step we take that helps to address the root cause of systemic inequities will influence change within the educational system.

We've all heard the belief: "Some students thrive while others don't." But focusing on individuals and communities is not the issue. When we prioritize fixing the individual, we risk putting them back into a bad environment. You can see the problem with the approaches in education. Interventions, recommendations, and strategies that we use to "fix kids" never work because then we put them right back into the system that didn't serve them in the first place. This is why certain students, like youth of color and those from high poverty communities, persistently have disproportionate outcomes. Systemic structures cause these inequities. Therefore, we need systemic solutions at the source.

We believe most educators want to make a difference and bring about positive change for their students and school community. The reality is educators work within these complex systems, which often seem toxic and immovable. The topics people often worry or complain about fall into three categories: things we can control, things we cannot control, and those outside of our control and influence. While systemic change is often out of our control, a strength-based approach allows you to focus on areas that are immediately within your sphere of control.

Think about what you have no direct control over. This might include decisions and activities within your political, social, organizational, or personal context; immovable project constraints (such as deadlines or budgets); and other people's attitudes, behaviors, or feelings. Let go of the things outside of your control so you can focus on where you can have the greatest impact. When you can let go of the areas you can't control then you can spend more of your time addressing the areas you have control over.

THE REFRAME:
OUR PROBLEMS EXIST WITHIN THE SYSTEM

Why do you think certain outcomes continue to persist? Seriously, take five minutes and list why you think certain outcomes persist for certain groups of students.

What did you come up with? As you reflect on the source of these issues, notice the source of the problem. Was it because of an inherent problem within the child? Was it because of their culture? *Why?*

Despite decades of research and recommended interventions, certain groups of students continue to have worse outcomes when compared to their peers. *But why?*

Research has documented patterns of disproportionality, as far back as 1968, with students who are minority, high-poverty, and receive special education services. Disproportionality is the over- or under-representation of a group compared to another group in a category. Historically, Black and Latinx students are more likely to be referred and receive special education services than students in other groups.

African American students (aged six to twenty-one) in special education services were twice as likely as their counterparts across all other groups to receive services for intellectual disability (ID) and two times more likely to be identified as having emotional disabilities (ED). In addition, 70 percent of the students who were identified as having an emotional disability were males.

But why?

Data has consistently revealed that racialized youth and students from high poverty communities have historically faced more challenges in school. In addition, research shows a correlation between poverty and academic outcomes. Students in poverty experience less success in school compared with their non-low-income, non-minority counterparts both with and without disabilities.

Behaviorally, youth of color—especially Black males—have historically been referred for disciplinary infractions at disproportionate rates compared to Caucasian students. These negative trends also connect to significantly higher rates of suspensions for youth of color. How many more research studies must exist to show that stressors such as poor nutrition, unsafe living conditions, and high crime rates are more likely to impact youth of color from high poverty communities? We know this. We can predict it, yet these unfair trends continue to persist. *But why?*

Why is it that children who live in persistent poverty are at higher risk for mental illness and in greater need of mental health treatment? Why are youth of color identified as deficient and "at-risk" for these disproportionate outcomes? Despite these persistent and alarming statistics, the academic, behavioral, and mental health needs of youth of color, students from high-poverty communities, and especially African American males are often characterized as being the sole source of their problems. Why is it that students who we can all predict at this point, who are historically under- and overrepresented in the data, are more likely to receive office discipline referrals, be removed from school, and have an increased risk of dropping out of school and entering into the juvenile justice system? *Why?*

We must stop blaming kids and look at solving the problems within the structures of our systems, beliefs, policies, and practices.

The belief that students are to blame and need fixing is erroneous and will continue to perpetuate these outcomes. Instead, it is imperative to examine *the why*. We must also examine the conditions that perpetuate these outcomes for certain students. We must stop blaming kids and look at solving the problems within the structures of our systems, beliefs, policies, and practices, which continue to produce these outcomes for certain groups of students. To understand *the why*, we must get at the groundwater of these problems.

We adopted the metaphor of the groundwater as a helpful way to understand the problem that exists within structures and not kids. Joyce James and Bayard Love first presented this metaphor in 2013. The metaphor aligns with inequity and structural racism.

Many people have difficulty understanding such concepts because of complex terminology, so the metaphor takes a complex concept and makes it easy to understand.

The simple story is about a young child who lives by a massive lake. Each morning, the child would walk past the lake and head to school. One day, the child saw one dead fish floating belly-up. The child thought, "Hmm. What's wrong with that fish?"

(Now, imagine the fish is a student failing in the educational system. We might say, "That child is lazy" or "That kid is bad.")

That same child walked outside the next day and noticed a group of dead fish floating belly-up.

The child said, "Hmm. What's wrong with that group of fish?"

(We might say, "What's wrong with those students from *that* neighborhood?" or "The apple doesn't fall far from the tree.")

The next day, the child walked outside and saw a large number of dead fish floating belly-up. The child finally said, "I wonder what's wrong with the water."

WHAT YOU CAN DO TOMORROW

Most of the water on the planet is not above ground. To understand why the fish aren't thriving, we have to understand there's some sort of contamination. A marine biologist would argue that to fix the contamination, you must identify the source below the surface—in the groundwater. Here are ways you can get to the groundwater of the systemic problems so you can help solve them.

- **Start within your sphere of control.** That means starting with yourself! Raise your self-awareness by identifying and understanding your uniqueness and strengths. To fully understand yourself, aim to recognize the impact and power of your thoughts, choices, conclusions, and assumptions. How does your thinking impact your actions? Create the space to intentionally shift your thinking.

- **Recognize what you can control.** What do you have control over? Regardless of your industry, title, or circumstances, this answer is consistent. Typically, the answer is "only ourselves"—our behaviors and attitudes. As the saying goes, "Your attitude determines your altitude."

- **Recognize what you might be able to influence.** Although we cannot control others, we can influence them. Increase your awareness of your behaviors so you can influence others more effectively. Even a small shift in your mindset or approach can create a far greater impact. Write down two or three areas you might be able to influence.

- **Recognize what you can't influence yet.** Systemic inequities may seem daunting to challenge and influence. Write down one or two areas you can't influence—yet!

- **Look for sources of contamination in your sphere of control.** It's okay to feel overwhelmed and lost as to where to start. Your school is a large, complex system, operating within a myriad of even larger and more complex systems. You can begin by using data (we go into greater detail in Reframe

3) to help you uncover patterns of disproportion-ality. As an example, a classroom teacher might examine trends in discipline data to see if certain groups of students receive harsher discipline. A psychologist might examine which students are referred for special education services more often than others. A school leader might examine school culture and climate data to identify potential sources of contamination.

A BLUEPRINT FOR FULL IMPLEMENTATION

Follow these steps to develop your skills in avoiding equity detours and taking action.

Step 1: Recognize inequity.

Recognizing inequities is an essential first step because some people might not be aware of systemic inequities and how they impact students, schools, and the broader school community. In education, recognizing inequities might include noticing subtle biases in learning material, social-emotional learning curricula, classroom interactions, classroom policies, and schoolwide practices.

So many of us in the classroom have heard those phrases: "She's a bad student," "She's lazy," or "He doesn't care." It's easy to blame students for our struggles as teachers, but it can also be counterproductive. When you can recognize how inequity is showing up, you can better equip yourself to respond to it.

Tune in to inequity by authentically listening to the needs of people through empathy interviews, which are the cornerstone of design thinking. By entering and understanding another person's thoughts, feelings, and motivations, we can understand their choices and behavioral traits and identify their needs. Once you can understand someone's needs, then you can recognize how inequity might be impacting them from their unique perspective.

Step 2: Respond to inequity.

When you can recognize inequities, you can respond to them. Earlier, we asked why certain outcomes continue to persist. Disproportionate outcomes persist due to a failure to respond to inequities, especially when they are immediate and pervasive.

Responding to inequities is crucial for rooting out contamination at the groundwater level. We showed you a simple and powerful way to respond to inequity. Did you catch it? Earlier, we posed the question—why? Asking why is a simple but powerful tool against inequity. You might notice that Black students are twice as likely to receive an office discipline referral in your school. At your next team meeting, you might simply ask why these disproportionate data exist? As a practice, ask why five times to get to the root cause. Here's an example.

Team leader: Our data shows that Black students in the seventh grade have the highest number of office discipline referrals.

You: But why do they have the highest number of referrals? (why #1)

Team leader: It appears that a group of students, who are most likely Black, are coming into first period and receiving referrals for being tardy.

You: But why is that group of students always late? (why #2)

Team leader: Because they have a longer bus ride compared to other students.

You: Okay, so if they have a longer bus ride, why are they receiving referrals for the bus being late? (why #3)

Team leader: Well, it's just the policy.

You: Why do we have a policy that disproportionately impacts students for an issue that's not their fault? (why #4)

Team leader: We've always had the tardy policy, but we never updated it after the boundaries changed.

You: Why hasn't the policy been updated since the boundary change? (why #5)

Team leader: We never considered it or who it might impact until now. Thank you!

In this example, you can see that the school disciplined a certain group of students due to a policy change. The leaders who made the policy change didn't consider the impact on that group, and it penalized students who had a longer bus ride. You were able to recognize and respond to an inequity immediately, and the team leader took action to immediately redress the inequity.

Step 3: Correct inequity.

Redressing inequities means correcting them. In the prior example, the team leader immediately took action to review the tardy policy, determine who was impacted by it, and create a tardy policy that is more equitable. When you see an inequity, immediately take action to correct it.

Step 4: Actively cultivate equity.

Aim to actively develop your knowledge, skills, and will to apply an equitable lens to everything you do and across every practice and policy in your school. Equity isn't an add-on or task we should force people to perform. Instead, equity is a process of ensuring every student has the access and opportunity to be successful. Systemize these practices by weaving them into the fabric of your school culture and community.

Step 5: Sustain equity.

Commit to doing what's right for children. You can sustain equity by making it a habit to consider who will be impacted positively and negatively by decisions and practices at the classroom, school, and district levels. By reflecting on those who are impacted by decisions, you will constantly look through a lens of doing what's right for children and maximizing the positive impact and minimizing the harm.

Another way to sustain equity is to engage students, staff, parents, and school leaders at key touchpoints. By constantly engaging with all people impacted by your decisions (as well as school or district decisions), you will be aware of potential barriers, instances of harm, and the needs of people. When you engage with people impacted by decisions, you gain valuable insight into what's working and not working. It also allows you to more quickly adapt to their needs and address their concerns. Finally, it opens the door for constant communication and feedback—a powerful tool to support equity.

It won't always be easy, and you may be met with criticism and pushback as you do this worthy work.

OVERCOMING PUSHBACK

To make real progress and improve student outcomes, we need changes that go beyond examining students at the individual level. We need systemic change. But systemic change is hard. The American education system is large and complex, which means resistant to change. Because changing a complex system involves influencing many smaller parts, people might believe meaningful change at the systemic level is unattainable. Here are a few common types of concerns for this Reframe and how to address them.

Systemic change is not possible. The word "impossible" says, "I'm possible." We recognize change is complex, and every system differs. We also recognize that the same inequities persist and negatively impact the same groups of people despite the system or industry. Therefore, we must unwaveringly believe that change is possible in our work, especially with young people, and view challenges as opportunities. You will start to see setbacks as setups for student success. Failure will take on a new meaning, and you will want to fail faster because you understand that the faster you fail, the more quickly you will reach a solution that works—and that leads to success. Most importantly, when you believe change is possible, you believe that every student you interact with has the potential to thrive.

We have to move at a pace that's comfortable for the majority. When a marine biologist notices contamination in the groundwater, they develop a plan to quickly and safely eradicate it. Similarly, when we notice contamination in the school system, we must develop a plan of action. Far too often, educators notice an injustice and won't do anything about it or will expect someone else to take action. When this happens, nothing gets done. Instead, we must develop a plan of action and execute it. A plan of action is just a paper or a spreadsheet—a plan with no action. The key is to *take action* as quickly as you can. In the context of inequity, we must move with a sense of urgency because our actions directly give children the access and opportunity to thrive. Here are a few questions to consider.

- Who will be impacted by the plan?

- Will the plan continue to perpetuate inequities?

- Might the plan create new inequities or exacerbate existing ones?

- Who will benefit, and who will be marginalized by the plan?

- Who has provided feedback on the plan (students, teachers, mental health staff, school leaders, parents)?

- Who else would be useful to provide feedback to make the plan even more effective?

The problem *does* exist within the child. You might also hear, "The child really is lazy" or "We get it, but the child really is bad." When you hear this type of deficit-thinking terminology in real time, you must address it at the moment. When someone says, "That child is lazy," you might reframe it as an executive functioning skill the child is developing. Specifically, you might say, "I've noticed the child engaging in a sustained activity for twenty minutes, so perhaps they're not lazy. I wonder if the child is developing their executive functioning skill of initiating tasks?" You might take it a step further and recommend some of your favorite strategies for initiating tasks, such as using a timer, frequent reminders, or simply providing step-by-step directions on what to do.

THE REFRAME IN ACTION

Dr. James Comer was the first African American to become a full professor at the Yale School of Medicine. He currently serves as the Maurice Falk Professor of Child Psychiatry at the Yale Child Study Center and the associate dean at the Yale School of Medicine. His pivotal research project paved the way for the eventual emergence of social-emotional learning. In 1968, Comer and his colleagues designed an intervention project for poor Black students attending two elementary schools in New Haven, Connecticut.

The student body was 99 percent Black at each elementary school, and almost all were poor. Each school ranked near the bottom in achievement and attendance within the district, and each school also had severe discipline and behavior concerns. Consequently, a 25 percent turnover rate evidenced the unhappiness of the staff. Comer described the parents of students as being depressed, distrustful, angry, and alienated. Many blamed the students, the teachers, and even the students' families for their poor performance.

Comer and his team strategized and examined ways to improve outcomes for poor Black students at each elementary school. He hypothesized that focusing on improving test scores alone would not result in a better school or increased academic achievement. Instead, he emphasized a focus on the "whole child," an approach centered on addressing the unmet needs of students, a practice that would lead to improved academic achievement.

This intervention project spanned from 1968 to 1980. Comer worked with a social worker, psychologist, and special education teacher to examine the relationship between students' experiences at home and school. At the core of this project, his team investigated how the relationship between a student's home and school impacts their academic achievement. It's important to note that this project derived from Comer's belief that a child's home life directly affected their development, which, in turn, impacted their education. In his seminal 1988 article, Educating Poor Minority Students, Comer stated:

> "I began to speculate that the contrast between a child's experiences at home and those in school deeply affects the child's psychosocial development. This, in turn, shapes academic achievement. The contrast would be particularly sharp for poor minority children from families outside the mainstream."

He believed that the failure to bridge the social and cultural gap between home and school was the root of poor academic performance by minority students from high poverty communities.

It was a systemic failure, not one inherent to the child or their family.

Comer recognized that as long as developmental and social issues were left unaddressed, any educational reform would have, at best, only limited benefits for poor minority youth. This context is essential, especially when considering racism, violence, segregation, and discrimination during the 1960s.

He recognized the systemic injustices experienced by youth of color, particularly those from high poverty communities, who didn't have the same educational, economic, and political opportunities. Moreover, he noticed and considered the harmful impact discrimination and segregation had on Black students. He believed addressing developmental issues of poor Black youth and the detrimental effects of structural racism and bigotry inflicted upon Black people would lead to a systemic way to improve outcomes for Black youth. This belief was the basis of the School Development Program he founded, with its focus on the link between social development and learning (sounds close to social-emotional learning, right?). Moreover, when you bring the two together, you can prevent, address, and resolve concerns.

The focus and approach of the School Development Program produced remarkable results. Within five years, the two schools, which initially ranked lowest in academic achievement across thirty-three elementary schools, rose to the top (ranked third and fourth). Also, students' attendance rates improved to first and second across the district. They also saw a significant reduction in behavior problems across both schools.

By the end of the project, academic achievement at each school had surpassed the national average. Truancy and disciplinary problems had significantly declined. Comer then replicated the success in more than fifty schools. According to Comer, the critical elements of success in the New Haven schools involved addressing systemic injustices; relentlessly collaborating with staff, parents, and the community; and figuring out the needs of the students.

His systemic approach to school transformation helped staff be sensitive to children's developmental needs. Staff in the New Haven schools also learned that achievement and behavior problems resulted primarily from unmet needs instead of intentional bad behaviors. The key takeaway is that Comer showed that the problem existed within the system and not the students. Perhaps more importantly, he and his team of researchers developed a systematic roadmap to improve outcomes for youth of color and students living in poverty.

Students are not to blame. The belief that students are to blame and need fixing is erroneous. This way of thinking only continues to perpetuate disproportionate outcomes. Instead of trying to "fix" poor-performing students, let's examine the structures and systems within schools that promote an inequitable system for educational attainment. Let's work together to fix the educational system in America and ensure equitable access for all children.

3

HUMANIZE YOUR DATA
Students Not Stats

If you think you know what a student, or group of students, needs or is like by a review of their educational records, challenge yourself to put that aside and get to know the student as an individual. It takes time, which I know we are always short on in education, but it is so worth it and is incredibly important if we truly want schools to be a place where we are part of a whole system that supports children to be their best selves.

— KRISTA RICE, SCHOOL PSYCHOLOGIST

THE BELIEF:
WE MUST QUANTIFY OUR DATA

L ET'S TALK ABOUT data. Every school system collects data. But the important question is "How do we use this data?"

- Is it used to check a box?

- To inform decision-making?

- To better understand the perspectives of our students and families?

- Or to blame our students and families?

The way we collect and interpret our data can either contribute to deficit thinking in our buildings or disrupt it.

Think about the data collected in your school building and your classrooms. Next, think about who looks at it. If someone *is* looking at the data, is it analyzed consistently? Critically? Do we collect more data if we don't have a solution to an identified problem? How can we use the already collected data to identify real patterns and solutions—without blaming our students?

For example, if we identify high suspension rates for a large group of students, do we interpret that as a deficit innate to that group of students? Or do we dig deeper to examine our policies and practices? Have we contributed to the presence (or our perception) of these behaviors?

Disparities in student outcomes plague our school systems year after year. Whether academic achievement data, school discipline data, special education data, or student dropout data, our schools continue to replicate the systemic inequities in our larger societies.

Why haven't we identified solutions yet?

Why aren't we digging deeper?

Why are we asking the same questions and continuing to implement the same "solutions" without involving the people directly impacted by our practices?

Because the reality is that any disparity in outcome for a group of students reflects something WE are doing wrong.

We argue that our current processes don't allow us to truly *feel* our data or what we are saying when we identify problems. If an administrator says, "Our bilingual students are disproportionately placed in restrictive special education classrooms at three times the rate of monolingual students," and there is no audible gasp in the meeting room, that is a problem!

Rather than accepting these disparities as the norm, we need to take accountability and resist the deficit narrative reinforced by our data patterns.

Data easily overwhelms teachers, who experience difficulty relating it to their practices. Why? Because our current data systems don't answer the right questions. We need data to inform our practices in our classrooms. Of course, we collect formal data on student assignment and test performance, attendance, and discipline, but are we taking the time to collect data on how our students FEEL? How do they feel about our approaches? How do they feel about their performance? This is the first issue.

Perhaps we are used to only valuing student performance and outcome data because it allows us to identify problems. But how can we address those problems if we don't know *why* they are happening? For example, let's say a classroom teacher identified a few students who continuously perform poorly on academic assignments. The data we collected (grades) identified the problem. But if we stop there, we are not using data appropriately. We need to go deeper. Regardless of the formal data we collect, all students have a perspective to share about what's working for them and what's not. As often as we administer a quiz to students, we should be gathering feedback from them to inform our approaches and practices.

Many school districts also only review their data patterns at key markers in the year. For example, a school team may review their outcome data at the end of the year to set goals for the next year based on identified problems. In some "progressive" schools, we may see an end-of-year survey. Regardless, the issue is that we are too late. By analyzing data from events that have already occurred, we missed the mark on effectively serving our students. We may have already harmed some students. Students represented in our data may move on to a new school. Many will return to our buildings in the fall with a negative perception of school because we did not catch and address our problems in action.

Deficit thinking also shows up in the language we use around data.

"Underperforming."

"At-risk."

"Low."

People use these words and phrases to describe whole groups of students who don't hit a predetermined benchmark. It dehumanizes our students and assumes that all students within a given category are the same—struggling. It doesn't acknowledge the individual student behind the data.

We see the same issue within our schoolwide data. We have "good" schools and "bad" schools. Why do we identify "good" schools by test scores, discipline rates, and attendance patterns rather than by students demonstrating critical thinking skills, confidence in their learning abilities, and feelings of belonging? An unconscious belief exists that our quantitative data tell the whole story, automatically equating "good-outcome schools" with supporting the whole child.

This method of thinking is harmful for several reasons. We often act like numbers are objective. ("The numbers don't lie.") However, when we use numbers, we are forced to think of some numbers as "right" and others as "wrong" with nothing in between. It also reinforces that when we identify disparities in performance data, it is the students' fault rather than the school's fault. Without telling the story behind the numbers, people fill in the blanks. Finally, it reinforces that Black, Brown, and Indigenous youth are problematic because their numbers aren't the same as White youth. Rather than critically examining what practices could lead to disparate numbers, we—once again—fill in the blanks. It is much easier to find fault within groups of people when we only view them as numbers.

Unfortunately, our current data processes place more value on numbers than on words or feelings. This is especially true when talking about academics. We frequently rely on reading scores that indicate what "grade level" a child is reading at and use this one data source to tell the whole story about a student's abilities. Worse—even if alternative data exists, test scores harbor much greater weight because they are "unbiased" and "fair." A student may read at a higher level than their score captures because of test anxiety. A parent may see them reading books of interest at home, but their in-class work shows a different ability level.

Many educational institutions forgot that test companies warned us about the dangers of using one piece of data to inform decisions about a student's abilities and educational needs. Yet, we continue in our efforts to make reading and other skills "easily measurable," leading to the deficit-based view of reading where some will be above others—and some will not measure up.

When you think about data like this, it's hard to understand why we continue to rely on numbers. Policymakers created a world where educators must place numbers on our student outcomes, all with the goal of "holding institutions accountable" for making positive changes. While it comes from good intentions, it conditions educators to see students not as individuals but as populations to be measured and monitored.

Funding and teacher evaluations depend on our numbers improving at specific rates, leading us to further rely on one sole source of data. This leads to a system where data-based decision-making cannot effectively occur. Our data is not accurate, comprehensive, meaningful, or used to better serve our students. It also fuels our current culture of high-stakes testing in schools, which intensifies the focus on student deficiencies—at the expense of addressing larger systemic inequities.

The fact is that the traditional outcome/quantitative data only identifies a broad potential problem. To identify the real problem, we must dig deeper. To implement solutions, we must go even deeper than that. We cannot dismiss the voices of our students. Our students are not lone numbers in a spreadsheet or graph. They are human beings with thoughts, feelings, emotions, and important contributions. We must capture that data to inform our educational practices.

When we only collect outcome data, our attempts to understand the "why" will always blame students for their shortcomings. When we attempt to address the "why" without taking the time to understand it directly from those impacted, we will always worsen inequities. And finally, when we only collect outcome data, we allow ourselves to revisit a narrative that everyone already knows and that everyone already feels unable to change.

So no, outcome data doesn't tell the whole story. We must stop numerizing the feelings out of ourselves and our students.

THE REFRAME:
HUMANIZE YOUR DATA

It's time for educators to shift from relying on what education experts Dr. Shane Safir and Dr. Jamila Dugan term "satellite data." We need "street data" that focuses on stakeholder input, student assets, and real solutions.

They describe satellite data as broad quantitative measures like test scores, attendance patterns, and graduation rates. While this information can identify trends and point adult attention toward inequities, that is about all it allows us to do. The data is rarely analyzed in real time, meaning that once professionals identify patterns, it is too late to make the data-based decisions that all schools strive to use data for. Satellite/outcome data justifies deficit thinking, leading to an emotional cycle of educators blaming subgroups of students for continuing to demonstrate poor data patterns. We have not taken a step back to identify or address the root causes.

By examining data without that context, we must guess about what is happening.

On the other hand, we can use street data (observational and experiential data that emerges directly from our students). Street data includes feelings about the learning environment and what might impact students' abilities to be successful. It seeks to iden- tify what's *right* in our students and schools rather than what's *wrong*. We identify solutions to our problems *directly from the source* and in *real time*. And even better—street data is always in front of us, just waiting to be interpreted.

For example, imagine a student is sent to the principal's office two days in a row for "disruptive behavior." We use an office dis- cipline referral for satellite/outcome data. It tells us nothing other than something the student was doing in one specific moment with one teacher (who perceived the actions as disruptive enough that the student needed to leave the room). When the student reaches the office, what happens? From your experience, do you feel that we are asking the right questions?

Imagine that the student receives a brief reprimand from the principal and returns to the classroom the first time. The student receives lunch detention and a call home the second time. Imagine that it happens again the next day. Now the school suspends the student. We have allowed our satellite data to speak for itself in this sequence of events rather than gathering street data that tells the whole story. We have not humanized our interactions with the student. We believe that we have "objective" and "concrete" data to back up the decisions we made. In this example, the student will return from the suspension, and nothing will have changed. However, people now view the student as the problem, and we have yet to identify a solution.

Imagine, alternatively, that the principal truly took the time to understand what happened according to the student. For example, the following questions might be asked:

- What happened from your perspective?

- What were you feeling at the time you showed that behavior in class?

- What led to those feelings?

- How do you usually get along with that teacher?

- What is the classroom dynamic, and what is your usual experience or feeling in this class?

- Do you perceive a problem with the situation that occurred in class and with your behavior?

And we can't just ask these questions and move on. We must continue until we truly understand the student's perception of the situation. Next, we seek to understand the teacher's account by examining the factors they believe led to the situation. Observations are conducted in this teacher's classroom and in another teacher's classroom to gain further context. Finally, we speak with the student's family (not to punish but to gain their perspective about the incident).

Cory Cain, dean of instruction at a school in Illinois, says, "My job is to be in the classroom, not at a desk; in the classroom watching these things happen. The first thing you would do is start taking data. You have to."

This doesn't have to be done solely by the principal or an administrator. We need school psychologists, school counselors, and school social workers as well. Imagine that the student shares that they "Already know everything the teacher is talking about," that they are "bored," and that when they tried to explain this to the teacher, the teacher viewed it as disruptive. Imagine that the teacher shared that they were teaching their lesson, and most students were engaged in it, but this student kept interrupting her and distracting classmates. Rather than dismissing one of their perspectives or giving more credence to the teacher's perspective, we take both into account and recognize that two things can be true at once.

This is where our quantifiable data misses the mark. It misses the humanness of our interactions. Imagine that when we speak to the family, they share that their child has been complaining about how boring this class is. They encouraged their child to tell the teacher that they aren't challenged enough. Imagine that we observe no issues with this student in any other classes.

Does this make the teacher wrong? No.

Does this mean we need to change the narrative? Yes.

By identifying what happened beneath our satellite data, we can determine what practices to change so we can prevent future problems. When our data reveals information about the student learning experience, teachers and other staff can check their assumptions about student learning. It identifies what Dr. Tim Runge, a school psychologist, calls a "problatunity"—in other words, "We've got a problem here, but it's an opportunity for us to ameliorate it."

When we embrace street data and develop a culture that values it, we commit to listening, observing, and seeking answers that identify root causes rather than assuming we know what's best. Safir and Dugan offer three types of street data:

1. **Artifacts**

   Anything created by a member of the school community that offers insight into the culture of its creator or community members.

   Examples: Student work, teacher-designed tasks, video or audio recordings of student/teacher discussions, and a professional learning agenda from a staff meeting.

2. **Stories/Narratives**

   The oral (and sometimes written) sharing of stories, histories, lessons, or other knowledge that maintains a historical record and sustains cultural identities.

   Examples: Interviews with families, case studies of students, oral histories of the community, identity maps created by students, journals from teachers or students, comment cards submitted after a lesson or meeting, and listening campaigns.

3. **Observations**

   The study of human behavior (e.g., interactions between students and teachers, interactions between administration and teachers, in various spaces in the school building) with an emphasis on both nonverbal and verbal communication.

   Examples: Equity participation trackers (such as tally participation in interaction by race, gender, etc.), meeting observation notes, and nonverbal observation notes.

Most importantly, you can get creative! Essentially, street data is any on-the-ground data that amplifies the perspectives of those at the "margins" of our school community. We'd like to highlight our favorite examples from Safir and Dugan in more depth—audio feedback interviews, equity participation trackers, student-led community walks, and fishbowls.

- *Audio feedback interviews.* After discovering a key equity challenge, conduct an audio-recorded focus group with students, parents, or community members to gain their perspective on what's happening. With participant permission, determine how to proceed after the interviews. You can make the data anonymous or keep it as is, transcribe it, highlight key themes collaboratively, and share the data at the next staff meeting to ground discussions. After presenting the data, encourage staff to identify key themes. You can also invite the participants to the staff meeting so they can emphasize the pieces that were most impactful for them and the themes they noticed.

- *Equity participation trackers.* When observing a classroom or school location, the observer tracks an identified behavior, such as by race/ethnicity, gender, EL/monolingual, special education/general education, or student grade. The behavior could be as simple as who is called on to participate. It could be as complex as the number of positive versus negative feedback forms. Present the collected data to all individuals present during the observation and facilitate a discussion. This method can be particularly powerful to uncover the biases of adults who believe they act fairly and equitably. It can allow for an impactful school cultural dissection and connection to broader patterns.

- *Student-led community walks.* A potentially powerful method of disrupting our deficit perspectives is to immerse ourselves in the community. To do this intentionally, allow the experience to be student-led. Next, invite the students to design a professional learning experience for educators that typically involves two afternoons—one for students to share their experiences in the community and one where staff members learn about important community sites, locations, or people. This experience flips the narrative on who is the expert, allows educators to gain a sense of values, and reframes what we believe to be true about our students versus what is true.

- *Fishbowls.* A fishbowl dialogue can publicly draw out the perspective of groups at the margins. Fishbowls typically involve a small group of people engaging in a discussion in the middle of a room while other participants encircle the group, listen, and jot down key themes. This can be especially powerful when inviting those with less power to participate in the discussion, while those with power sit and listen. Fishbowls are best implemented when a key equity issue has been identified that impacts a specific group of people. Discussions should focus on sharing personal experiences, thoughts, ideas, and needs. They can involve teachers, students, parents, paraprofessionals, and community members. Most central to a successful fishbowl is a willingness to listen, even when it's hard.

Every time we collect meaningful data from our students, we reinforce the idea that humanized data is valid—chipping away at the deficit narrative of our traditional data sources telling the whole story.

We gain much insight from humanized data. Andrea Davis, an education researcher, references a teacher who insists she doesn't need district reading scores to know her students' reading abilities. Rather, she states, she listens to them. She listens to how they talk about their reading experiences, watches their reactions to what they read, and notices who they are as learners and as people. This teacher emphasizes that this form of "data collection" does so much more than a standardized score could—it builds the relationships and connections students need to learn with their teachers. Knowing our students, acknowledging what they bring to our classrooms, and listening to them can provide data about how they read and write, what meaning they make from schooling, and where their strengths lie. We are moving from evaluating our students to valuing their experiences.

WHAT YOU CAN DO TOMORROW

There are some straightforward ways to collect and use street data. Here, we present actions you can take right away in your classrooms and schools:

- **Broadly reflect on the data you already collect.** Can you identify potential "problatunities" when examining your data from an anti-deficit approach that focuses on your practices and procedures? What questions do you still have? Take note of these questions and consider bringing them to light with your students to see what they think.

- **Check out your publicly available data.** Every state education organization publicly offers data about their school districts. If you can't find the right data at the state level, you can surely find federal data. What historical patterns can you identify within your school or district? What opportunities for street data collection come to mind? Who could you collaborate with to start brainstorming?

- **Examine how often you have solicited student feedback.** What decisions could you start involving your students in deciding? Maybe it's how much time you dedicate to a certain aspect of the learning experience. Perhaps it's how quickly you've been going through the material. Maybe it's opportunities for students to participate or work in groups. Adults make many decisions about student experiences without receiving input from the students. Why not see what happens when we ask them? Some suggestions may involve simple adjustments that make a tremendous impact.

- **Student daily check-ins and check-outs.** Many schools use check-in/check-out (CICO) as a reactive behavior intervention rather than a proactive means of collecting information about students' feelings. Checking in and out with all your students every day or every week is an excellent way to understand how students are feeling, what they need, and what you can do differently in real time as a teacher. This is street data! It can involve student completion of a daily Likert scale (where responders choose their level of agreement with a statement, usually on a scale of 1–strongly disagree to 5–strongly agree), a brief sentence, or even a daily verbal check-in and check-out. What makes this street data is how you *use* the data.

- **Ask your students.** As Dr. Runge says, "There's no reason why a teacher can't solicit feedback from their students at key markers along the way." Simply ask them for feedback.

- **Administer a short feedback survey to your students.** You can use a one-time survey if you're interested in examining a specific topic. It can also serve as a pre/post survey to determine the impact of a new practice or a monthly check-in to see how your students feel about your practices and their progress.

- **Ask your school psychologist.** Chances are that your school psychologist has been waiting to be involved in supporting your classroom practices. If you have identified a "problatunity," consider collaborating and brainstorming with your school psychologist and asking them to aid you in collecting street data.

A BLUEPRINT FOR FULL IMPLEMENTATION

So, what does this look like in practice? Based on all these ideas, we present a data process that allows us to shift away from deficit thinking by identifying proactive solutions directly from the source. We call this the HUMANE approach, and it stands for Highlight, Unpack, Magnify, Analyze, Normalize, and Evaluate.

STEP 1: ## H – HIGHLIGHT YOUR SATELLITE DATA AND HOME IN ON YOUR "PROBLATUNITIES."

Begin by reviewing traditional satellite data. Start with available data around student opportunities and outcomes. Such data can exist at the school level (suspension patterns, schoolwide test scores) or the classroom level (participation rates, scores on assignments). We can often easily identify where our problems lie by broadly looking at data. Other times, we may feel the need to quantify the challenges. This is where it may make sense to calculate what school psychologists Michael Boneshefski and Tim Runge call *risk indices* and *risk ratios*.

A *risk index* is the proportion of a group at risk for a specific outcome. It determines the proportion (or percentage) of students who have achieved a certain outcome or been on the receiving end of one. You calculate this number by dividing the total number of students from a subgroup that has received an outcome divided by the total number of students from that subgroup.

Risk ratios allow us to examine the risk of a certain outcome occurring for a subgroup of students compared to the same outcome for a different group. To calculate a risk ratio, you divide the risk index for a subgroup of students by the risk index for the comparison group. A risk ratio of 1.0 indicates that the outcomes are the same. Above 1.0 indicates overrepresentation, and one below 1.0 indicates underrepresentation.

Consider the following example from author Dr. Kelsie Reed's dissertation:

If there are seventy-five Black students enrolled in a school, and thirty-seven of those students have received at least one suspension, the risk index would be .49 (37/75). This means that 49 percent of Black students within the school have received at least one suspension. To understand what this means, we must compare it with White students at the same school. If there are two hundred White students enrolled in the same school, and forty of those students have received at least one suspension, the risk index would be .20 (40/200). This means that 20 percent of White students within the school have received at least one suspension.

If the risk index for Black students receiving a suspension is .49 and the risk index for White students receiving a suspension is .20, this indicates overrepresentation. The Black students appear to be 2.47 (.49/.20) times as likely as White students to receive a suspension.

What is important here is that even though *more* White students have been suspended than Black students in total (forty White students; thirty-seven Black students), we need to take into account the total numbers of both Black and White students, not just the number of suspensions. That is why risk ratios are helpful in seeing the extent of disparities.

Risk ratios can also identify participation disparities. For example, what is the risk of our Latinx students participating in extracurricular activities compared to our White students? If the number is not 1.0, we have identified the "problatunity" of under or overrepresenting groups of students in school-offered opportunities.

We must also calculate the risk ratios of teacher practices. For example, what is the risk of one teacher sending a student to the office compared to another teacher? When we think about our satellite data in terms of both student and teacher behaviors, we begin examining the reasons for over and underrepresented students. See Image 3.1.

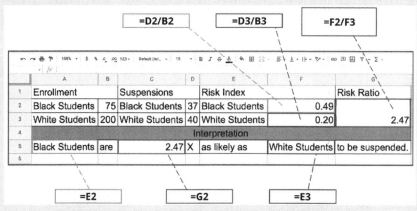

Image 3.1: Calculating risk indices and risk ratios in Google Sheets.

Perhaps your goal is to improve outcomes for the entire school building or an entire classroom. While you can calculate risk ratios at the school building level by comparing outcomes to other schools or districts (sometimes it's easier to identify the severity of practices this way), you only *need* to identify which outcome you want to improve at this point.

STEP 2: U – UNPACK THE PROCEDURES AND RULES AT PLAY.

After identifying the focus area, it's time to brainstorm and identify potential contributors to the problem. This is where teams are most likely to catch themselves engaging in deficit thinking. We encourage you to think only about the factors within your control—and not just the easily identifiable ones. We mean the culture, norms, and values assigned to different behaviors within our school. You must critically examine all school factors that contribute to the outcome.

For example, suppose you decide to focus on office discipline referrals. Consider the following:

- Examine the procedures that allow for an office discipline referral to happen.

- Is there a set of criteria that outlines when to institute a referral and when not to?

- What options do teachers have aside from referring students to the office?

- What behaviors are teachers most likely referring students for?

- Are there specific students being referred the most?

- Are there specific teachers doing most of the referring?

- What do teachers and students gain from referring students to the office?

- Essentially, what role does this practice play in our schools, and what is the outcome?

Academically, let's imagine you focus on a disproportionate number of Black students having scored lower on a standardized reading assessment. Again, we are not focusing on the student. Think about what the reading assessment measured and examine how those skills were taught. Reflect on student engagement with these concepts during the lesson.

As Cain said, "I see data, and I go, 'Oh wow, this child has a lot of Fs. Cool. Let's look at your processes. What are you doing?' Because that, to me, is a result of something that's happened in the classroom. I want to see your units; I want to see your chosen standards. I want to see the target goals you've created. I want to see any pre-assessment you gave the child to see what they already know."

To dig even deeper, determine how Black students seem to feel in that classroom.

- Do they feel safe?

- Do they feel cared for enough to express when they need help?

- Do they feel that their teacher cares about them as humans?

In essence, what factors impact your Black students' learning experiences? And finally, what is the impact of this disproportionate outcome? Again, you need to *feel* your data to understand its extent.

This process encourages staff to think critically about student outcomes. It aids in humanizing the process by examining why we do the things we do in schools and the impact of our behaviors. It reminds us of the power of intentionally using data to unpack our biases. The possible directions are endless when we examine our data in this way.

This process may also lead you to a different "problatunity" than you began with. For example, you may enter this step focusing on high rates of office discipline referrals and ultimately realize that the actual problem is a lack of teacher awareness of alternatives. Or you may begin focusing on standardized reading scores and realize that the problem is the assessment itself or how you're using the results. These shifts are good because they often indicate an even greater shift away from internal deficits.

Importantly, this is where many teams stop. They feel they have identified potential causes and are ready to implement solutions. However, questions will always be left unanswered if we stop there. While it may seem as if you are identifying causes in this step, the ultimate purpose is to identify what street data you still need to collect and why. What questions can you still not answer? We'll give you a hint—any instance where you assumed how a student or group of students felt is a question you can't answer. We can't assume what students or families need. We must ask them. We need to remove any deficit-based assumption from our vocabulary and involve those directly impacted by such assumptions in our thought processes. See the Appendix for a list of questions to help you unpack your school's procedures and rules.

STEP 3: M – MAGNIFY THE VOICES OF THOSE IMPACTED.

Who better to ask these questions than our students and families? Here is where we truly deviate from traditional data collection approaches. Rather than blaming the harmed students, we seek out their perspectives. We seek to understand where we have gone wrong. We seek their perspectives because if we don't, we will continue to make decisions rooted in bias and deficit thinking. We can magnify voices in several ways. It can be formal (through interviews, focus groups, and open-ended forms or surveys) or informal (brief conversations in the hallway, anonymous comment boxes placed throughout the building, and quick phone calls home). The goal is to magnify, not condemn or criticize. Seek the perspectives of those at the "margins," as Safir and Dugan say—individuals or groups of people who are most unheard and likely most instrumental in solving equity challenges.

One important idea to emphasize at this level is why you seek these answers. In our traditional schooling, we have many toxic power dynamics (see Reframe 7) that lead to a culture where students or families are, rightfully, afraid to share their true perspectives. If this is the case, you may need to take a few steps back to examine the culture of your school as a contributor to whatever outcome you originally examined.

Inform students and families about the identified data patterns. If there are disparities by race, ability, sexuality, gender, or social class, you must tell them. Won't it upset them, you ask? Perhaps— but what will upset them more is if you don't involve them and continue harming them. When you share that this is a problem you've identified and are determined to solve, you can all work together to understand why it's happening.

The approach is also incredibly important. If you conduct observations or interviews cold and transactionally, you are not collecting true street data. Often, this phase is uncomfortable because you must listen to potentially uncomfortable perspectives without becoming defensive. However, when you approach this phase from a stance of compassion, curiosity, and empathy, it can be incredibly powerful in disrupting assumptions and harmful narratives. It allows you to view the numbers as referring to humans with feelings, beliefs, assets, worries, and valid opinions. It allows you to see through their eyes. It likely challenges many of the plans you originally discussed as a team. That opens the door for creative solutions.

> While it can feel uncomfortable to implement new strategies, *the ones you've been relying on don't work.*

While we're dedicating most of the examples in this Reframe to the voices of students and families, we must also consider those working within the building who are often not involved in decision-making, such as paraprofessionals, cafeteria workers, and custodians.

STEP 4: A – ANALYZE YOUR DATA, ACCEPT RESPONSIBILITY, AND ADDRESS THE ISSUES.

This may be the most important step of the process. Begin by discussing what it was like to collect the street data. Discuss what patterns you predict to see in the data. Practice vulnerability.

You must treat the street data with as much integrity and value as other data sources, even if it challenges your perspectives, original assumptions, or traditional ways of doing things. All of it matters, and you need to consider all of it as you identify solutions. This step also requires you to *feel* your data. Learn to feel the voices of your community and the solutions they are offering.

This step also requires a willingness to deviate from tradition. When you seek input from historically dismissed people, you challenge systemic practices. While it can feel uncomfortable to implement new strategies, *the ones you've been relying on don't work.* When you frequently remind yourself of this, you open your mind to new approaches.

Another important facet of this stage is the continued involvement of those at the "margins." We need to welcome the stakeholders into this conversation as co-designers and co-dreamers (terms by Safir and Dugan). This holds us accountable for following up on our learning and ensuring that the meaning we have made from our data collection is accurate. We can encourage our community to challenge us and intervene if we have misunderstood something.

STEP 5: N – NORMALIZE THIS PROCESS.

This process is not a one-time act. In an ideal space, we will constantly upgrade it, both formally and informally.

Cain says that his students spend a lot of time giving their opinions about what's happening in the classroom. He has experienced firsthand the impact of gaining student perspective as an important means of data collection. He shared that he relies on the triangulation of three data sets—academic data, social-emotional data, and data from a student experience survey. His process implies that data collection is ongoing and incorporated into the school culture, ever informing the direction of school practices.

Another way to normalize this process is to truly walk the walk. Administrators and school leaders must continuously invest in coaching, professional development, and other resources designed to challenge assumptions made about students based on broad satellite data. This process begins to feel normal after continuous talks about this approach to data collection. It requires continuous support in efficiently engaging at the schoolwide and classroom levels. Teams must be willing to hold each other accountable for making sense of the data in an anti-deficit manner. School leaders must constantly remind the team that the data analysis goal is to improve instruction, student outcomes, and connectedness. It is not used to blame students or talk about supposed deficits.

Normalize feeling our data, being vulnerable, and validating the experiences of students.

We need to drastically change the perceived purpose of data collection. People did not design data to check a box. We collect it with clear, direct, and intentional goals to support our students in meaningful ways. We look at the whole student as a vibrant and ever-changing human being with important contributions to make. We look at our families as rich and informative sources of information about the strengths and needs of our students. We look at our data to find out what we need to do differently to better *see* our students and families.

STEP 6: E – EVALUATE YOUR EFFORTS COLLABORATIVELY.

When adopting new procedures and processes, continue to solicit feedback from your stakeholders. Review both satellite and street data to determine the right path. The beauty of this process is that it's never over. Because street data can be collected and addressed on the spot, this entire process could occur within one school day. And it's simple to evaluate our efforts when we've involved our students all along. They already know what outcome we are collaboratively trying to address. If it's working, we'll know—because they'll tell us.

OVERCOMING PUSHBACK

Oftentimes, it's hard to imagine changing our practices, especially when these changes involve more work or reach uncharted territory. Because our systems have always valued a certain type of "data" over others, you may find yourself pushing back against this change. Here are some thoughts you may find yourself or others getting stuck in, along with tips to push through the discomfort.

I can't look at my data in this way. This is a fair assumption at first glance. As educators, we often feel incredibly overwhelmed and at our breaking points, having been overtasked. When you feel that you can't do this alone, remind yourself that you don't *have* to do this alone. The entire street data framework depends on collaboration between the school community. You can enlist the help of your friendly school psychologist, counselor, or social worker, and you can incorporate your data analysis into your instruction with students. There are many nontraditional ways to ensure that you are looking at your data with a critical eye. And finally—remind yourself that this process will make your life easier in the long run!

I'm struggling with thinking about my contributions to the problem. This is also fair. Our deficit thinking automatically absolves us from responsibility. One way to approach this is to get vulnerable with yourself and use "I feel," "I think," or "I assume" statements. For example, you may "think" your students are bored. This paves the way for you to confirm or disconfirm this thought. This is a simple reframe, but when you add these phrases to the beginning of any root cause you identify, you begin to think about how you directly or indirectly contribute to something. Or better yet—it's an easy way for you to check your biases and assumptions about your students.

I don't have time to receive input like this from my students. Again, it may seem like this is the case. However, this process can be as simple as adding one question at the end of your quiz that reads: "How do you feel about the quiz you just took?" Use that data to inform how you interpret student performance on the quiz, what direction you need to go next, and changes you can make to your instructional approaches. Many teachers have warm-up activities at the beginning of the day. That could be an excellent time for check-ins, especially if you have identified a concern in your data. Consider using one warm-up per week to focus on "critiquing the classroom." You could bring a piece of data to your class, or your students can bring up their concerns. Not only are you helping students learn how to problem solve and advocate for themselves, but you're also humanizing them—and yourself—in the process.

The parents in my school already seem so busy. While this may also be true, we often don't give our parents enough meaningful opportunities to contribute. When we only contact them during the school day, we limit their ability to contribute. When we only contact them via one method (email, phone), we limit their ability to contribute. This leads to the deficit thought that our families are "too busy." However, when we meet them where they are, we can more readily involve them. Consider simply asking your families two questions: 1) What is the best day and time to reach you? and 2) What is the best method to reach you? Once you've identified these, you can figure out how to best involve them when collecting street data. Most parents will be ecstatic to know that we are interested in learning more about them and their needs.

THE REFRAME IN ACTION

Here's an example of a teacher implementing the HUMANE data approach in their classroom. It took place in a seventh grade classroom in a racially and ethnically diverse school. The teacher, Ms. Clark, was new to this role but previously served as a paraprofessional for several years. Her experiences were primarily at the elementary level, and this was her first time working with middle schoolers. She is White and in her mid-thirties. Her students represented a range of diverse racial backgrounds (Black, White, Latinx, Asian), which also reflected the school. Because she was a paraprofessional for special education students in her previous role, her principal tasked her with serving many of the students receiving push-in and pull-out special education supports. Most of these students were identified with a specific learning disability (SLD). She also had a few students who received English Speakers of Other Languages (ESOL) services, with Spanish being the most prevalent native language.

The classroom in question was her homeroom class, which she saw two times per day—at the beginning of the day, which led into reading instruction, and at the end of the day for writing and afternoon homeroom. In her building, morning homeroom is thirty minutes, and it's dedicated to breakfast and warm-up activities; afternoon homeroom is thirty minutes, and it's dedicated to homework or additional support.

At a recent professional development session, teachers in Clark's building learned about the HUMANE approach to data collection. The school encouraged them to implement it within their classrooms. Clark decided to accept the challenge because she struggled with her classroom management throughout the year. She started the process in mid-January. She felt that she knew her students fairly well, but there had been a recent uptick in "disruptive" behavior—leading to a subsequent uptick in her feeling the need to send students to the office.

She realized that she'd begun to "expect" the behaviors to occur from her "high fliers," and she found herself reducing students to this deficit. She met her breaking point with two female students who got into a physical altercation during a group activity, leading to a three-day suspension for both. She decided she needed to change her approach without blaming the students for the frustrating behavior she was continuously observing.

Clark began with her satellite data, and she focused mainly on her office discipline referrals throughout the year, calculating risk ratios where necessary. She identified the following "problatunities":

1. The students most likely to be referred to the office were Black female students.

2. When she examined further, she realized that the students were also disproportionately identified with an SLD. She quantifies the following concern: Black female students with learning differences are four

times as likely to be referred to the office from her classroom compared to White female students.

3. She unfairly referred her Black female students for disruption compared to other students.

4. In examining the work completion tendencies of those referred most often, she realized that the students most likely to be referred were also most likely to turn in incomplete work or none at all.

5. She had referred little to no students at the beginning of the year, but the referrals had been rapidly increasing, specifically during the reading block.

Clark began to examine all the factors impacting students before she sent them to the office. She caught herself engaging in deficit thinking on numerous occasions. For example, she began to think that if her students would just behave, she wouldn't have to send them to the office. That led her to think about what happens right before her students disrupt her lesson. She realized she had no idea what led to fighting or disruptive behavior.

She reflected on the following:

1. What does "disruption" mean to me?

2. What is the school's policy for office referrals?

3. What is my classroom management style?

4. What does my relationship with students look like?

5. What is my typical instructional approach and my classroom structure?

6. Are my students feeling disrupted by the same behaviors I consider disruptive?

7. What does "disruption" mean to my students?

8. How do my students feel about my classroom practices?

She realized that while she could answer some of the questions, only her students could answer others.

Clark collected multiple sources of street data from her students. She began by dedicating her homeroom to "data collection." She moved classroom desks into a circle and became vulnerable with her students by sharing the satellite data and "problatunities" she identified. She talked about the rise in discipline referrals, and she shared the disparities she'd noticed in her practices. She encouraged her students to share any thoughts about the data. Four students contributed their perspectives, where she learned that most students felt as if she treated her students of color differently than her White students. Ms. Clark found this difficult to process. She decided to ask the school psychologist to help determine which direction to go next. The school psychologist offered to conduct a few equity participation tracker observations where he focused on Clark's interactions with students by race.

In the meantime, Clark asked the five students (four were Black female students, one was a Latina student) she originally deemed her "high fliers" to participate in a series of recorded focus groups during lunchtime to gain their perspectives. All five students agreed to participate and shared that they were okay with the rest of the class knowing they had participated. To prepare for the groups, she tasked all the students in her class with developing some questions to include.

Finally, Clark conducted recorded interviews with the parents of three of the students from her focus groups. Students also participated in designing some of the questions she asked.

Clark approached all focus groups and interviews with an open mind, empathic stance, and anti-deficit demeanor. Her questions focused mostly on getting to know her students and parents on a deeper level, understanding their perspectives on education, and gaining a sense of what they value. She eventually asked about the office discipline referrals, stating that she was trying to learn how to better support her students. She asked each student and parent to share their perspective of what had happened in her classroom and why.

She used three sources of street data. She had the transcripts from her student focus groups, transcripts from her parent interviews, and observation data from the school psychologist.

The student focus group data revealed many complexities she hadn't considered. She identified the following themes.

Her students of color (specifically her female students of color) did not feel connected to her. They shared that from their perspective, whenever there was an issue, they were the ones blamed, even if another student triggered their behaviors. They collectively felt that Ms. Clark was not doing a good job of hearing them out.

They perceived her instructional methods as "boring." They also collectively agreed that there was too much teacher-led instruction and not enough opportunities to collaborate with their peers.

The students struggled to connect to the district-mandated books they read as a class. Clark noticed that the books did not offer much diversity in voice or experience.

Most shockingly, many of the behaviors she deemed problematic were not perceived as bothersome by her students. They spoke in depth about what "disruption" meant. Clark shared that when students didn't raise their hands before speaking, she perceived it as disrespectful and disruptive. While her students agreed this could be true while Ms. Clark was talking, they didn't perceive it as disruptive if Clark was not talking. Many instances challenged Clark's perception of "disruptive" behavior.

Results of the parent interviews highlighted a few other considerations. Most importantly, all three parents shared that their children had never been referred to the office this much before. One parent was upset because the school had never suspended her child until that year. They were all led to speak about their children's strengths, touching on many qualities Clark didn't even know that the students were interested in. She learned that one student who seemed to hate reading read many comic books at home. Ultimately, she discovered a lot of data that chipped away at her deficit beliefs.

The equity participation tracker revealed that while Clark did a good job of calling on most students equitably, the positive and negative responses and body language were discrepant by race. More specifically, she was more likely to offer a phrase such as "not quite" when a Black student responded and more likely to approve of White student contributions. When behaviors occurred, the school psychologist noted that Clark appeared hyper-focused on a group of students who (in his opinion) did not seem to be any more disruptive than the rest of the students in class.

Upon being presented with all this rich data, Clark started to grasp the magnitude of her practices. She shared the results with her students and co-led multiple brainstorming sessions with the school psychologist and her students to identify possible solutions.

They collaboratively developed a behavior contract that every student agreed on and signed. This contract outlined what behaviors were distracting in class and how the students and teacher would all hold each other accountable.

Clark continued the circle format for her morning homerooms and tasked volunteer students with designing and implementing activities to promote community within the room.

She instituted a student feedback system to allow students to share anything with her (either anonymously or openly), and she followed up with each data source as necessary. Then she began switching up her teaching methods—offering more opportunities for group work and other collaborative approaches.

Clark started each reading period with time for students to silently read any book of their choice, allowing them to bring in materials from home. She also allowed students to submit book suggestions to add to her classroom library for free reading time.

Any time a "disruptive" behavior occurred, the students and Ms. Clark collaboratively agreed that the student or students would be encouraged to share what happened (from their perspective) in the hallway with a plan to correct the behavior. Clark had made this possible with her new instructional approaches that were collaborative rather than group-led. She didn't feel that she missed content by stepping outside to speak with a student while the other students continued working.

Clark collaborated with the school counselor, who had implemented discussions about racism and microaggressions in the past with students, and she asked for help to design new ways to broach these topics with her students so she could learn from them.

Many of Clark's responses naturally led to this data collection process. She now solicits anonymous or open feedback from her students at any time. If she identifies a new trend in her satellite data, she follows up on it. In addition, her willingness to be vulnerable in the first place reiterated to her students that they could bring up things like this with her and expect that she would openly listen.

Clark and her students also decided to continuously check in about the new practices, any changes they needed to make, and any new problems. The shared ownership with everyone holding each other accountable aided Clark in truly understanding and seeing her students' behaviors change in real time.

Humanizing our data provides a powerful new method to examine the needs of our students. The more readily we garner such feedback and input in thoughtful ways, the easier it will be to disrupt the deficit ideologies our current data systems reinforce. As Alma Rosario, a school psychologist, says, "Change cannot happen without working with the families and children [we] serve."

How will you humanize your data?

THINKING, BELIEVING, AND FLOURISHING

WE CAN HACK DEFICIT THINKING
Connecting the Dots

The most impactful thing you can do is learn to notice and name deficit thinking. It is pervasive and is normal for those thoughts to come up. ... But we can work every day to notice and name these thoughts and actively push back on them. It is a daily practice, and we will have to work to reframe these throughout our careers.

— SHANNON WILLIAMSON, LEARNING RESOURCE CENTER DIRECTOR

THE BELIEF:
WE CAN'T DEFEAT DEFICIT THINKING

WE CAN'T DEFEAT deficit thinking.

It's too pervasive.

It's been the dominant way of thinking for centuries.

At a basic level, a deficit is a shortage or deficiency. In the context of education, deficit thinking is a harmful and outdated approach to schooling that involves either consciously or unconsciously blaming a student, a student's family, or a student's culture for academic or behavioral difficulties. Deficit thinking is a cognitive and emotional bias that can have serious consequences leading to students feeling inadequate as learners.

It also reinforces negative stereotypes about particular cultures. These experiences can be damaging for students and can impact their educational outcomes. Perhaps even worse, many people might be unaware of the role their deficit thinking plays.

An essential belief of deficit ideology is that inequities result from intellectual, moral, cultural, or behavioral deficiencies inherent in disenfranchised individuals and communities. It's a way to rationalize why some kids fail and others succeed. Deficit ideology assumes (incorrectly and unjustly) that marginalized people deserve marginalization because they are less intelligent, moral, or hardworking than privileged people.

When the term describes a person, community, or institution, people usually view it as much more than that. Deficit thinking says that *people* are deficient, and it blames their struggles on those deficiencies. Using deficit thinking to describe people on the losing end of existing power structures suggests that the problems aren't in the dominant systems but exist within the *people* in those systems.

Deficit thinking is a belief—a dangerous belief. Alma Rosario, a school psychologist, calls it "life-threatening." It's a dangerous belief that explains and justifies inequitable outcomes—such as standardized test scores or levels of educational attainment, for example—by pointing to supposed deficiencies within historically marginalized individuals and communities. It's believed that underserved students don't have the cognitive bandwidth, drive, or motivation to perform on par with their more privileged peers. Deficit thinking sends a clear message: If you are not doing as well as your fellow students, it is because there is something wrong with *you*.

It's a concept that has pervaded modern education. It manifests in messaging such as:

- "You're failing because you don't try hard enough."
- "You're not doing well because you're not good at this subject."
- "You don't belong here."

When you think about it this way, deficit thinking is particularly insidious. It expects historically marginalized students to work harder, be better, and achieve more to experience the same educational outcomes as their peers. It ignores the fact that they often fight against systemic disadvantages that their classmates typically don't have to overcome.

While it's easy to see why this kind of thinking is troubling, it's much harder to identify deficit thinking in action. Even worse, it conceals itself in a way educators may or may not observe. It's systematic and often invisible. It is challenging to defeat invisible things.

For example, you may struggle to understand how your thinking can impact your students. You feel like you treat all your students the same. How could any negative thoughts you have possibly impact your students when you practice patience and do your best to treat your students equitably? The issue is that deficit thinking is so pervasive that *we don't even realize when we're doing it.*

We all have biased beliefs and thoughts. It would be harmful to believe that we are not susceptible to the same thinking about students. In addition, the more you try to push away any negative thoughts you hold about your students' abilities, the more they come out in your actions. And research shows that even if we never say it out loud, our students know what we believe. As Cory Cain states, "Deficit thinking develops into a 'muscle memory' for students affected, meaning that they embody the low expectations that educators have for them."

Similarly, Shannon Williamson says, "Deficit thinking fuels academic anxiety. It makes it really hard for [students] to communicate with their instructors or seek help because deficit thinking just puts so much shame and stigma on the student. Students start to take on some of those deficit beliefs about themselves and feel that nothing can help them."

So, how can we defeat something so powerful when we don't even know it's a problem? As Curt Dudley-Marling and Paul Gorski (two deficit thinking experts) have researched and proposed—to counter deficit thinking, we need a much more persuasive narrative. You have the power to hack deficit thinking.

Psychologists wrote this book, so we can help you understand how your thinking, feelings, and behaviors are connected and work together to support or damage your students. Many psychologists use a framework called cognitive behavioral therapy (CBT) to support clients in understanding how their thoughts, feelings, and behaviors are connected. It is most beneficial for people struggling with cognitive distortions.

Cognitive distortions are inaccurate and irrational thoughts, perceptions, or beliefs that we unknowingly reinforce over time. These patterns of thinking can influence our feelings and emotions, and if not addressed and corrected, they can lead to pervasive deficit thinking.

These biased thought patterns convince us that something is either true or false. That impacts the way we behave when those thoughts are activated. Deficit thinking often shows up in the presence of such distorted thinking. While most psychologists argue that we all have cognitive distortions, some people may find themselves falling into the same traps over and over. When cognitive distortions persistently interfere with our happiness and well-being, they contribute to anxiety, depression, and other mental health concerns.

To conceptualize deficit thinking as cognitive distortions, think about a moment when you made an assumption that turned out to be wrong. Maybe it was a situation with a friend. You concluded that they were mad at you for something, but that ended up not being the case. Or maybe it was a project at work, and you thought your boss would fire you for making a mistake. Instead, they said they appreciated your diligence in bringing the problem to their attention. These are called cognitive distortions.

We've coined the term "deficit distortions" because they are based on multiple factors and show up in our classrooms in many ways. After working in the education field for many years, we often become desensitized to the humanity of our work. We develop distortions to sustain us as a coping mechanism. These distortions attach to anything—our beliefs and perceptions about education, stereotypes we've been primed to believe, or perceived failures we've experienced when we tried to support struggling students. We even validate our beliefs when we solely put our energy into our "high-performing" students, thinking they thrive because of us. For example, such beliefs may lead us to accept the poor performance of perceived "at-risk" students or show less praise for their work. Or you may call on these students less often than the students you assume already know an answer.

Although our distortions began as a coping mechanism, they harm our self-worth—and ALL our students. They impact our direct interactions with students, but they also impact the learning environment and classroom cultures we cultivate. And because every decision we make is rooted in our thinking patterns, distorted thinking patterns create a harmful impact.

As Cain states, "Your decisions are going to affect the child, right? Like, 'I'm going to move on in the curriculum,' 'I'm going to remain in the curriculum,' 'I'm going to switch the curriculum,' and 'I'm going to not be so rigorous.' Those decisions can affect the child, right? That's because of your mindset."

In this example, Cain connects our thoughts to our behaviors, which we determine by our beliefs about student needs. The connection: the more you allow your deficit distortions to rule your life, the more your student outcomes will reflect your distorted expectations, reinforcing these beliefs. We must stop this cycle.

As Karin Dykeman, an assistant professor of education, states, "Teachers' perceptions have been shown time and time again to have an overwhelming influence on student outcomes; what we believe is what they become. We literally influence the course of students' lives by choosing to believe they are capable or incapable."

How can we ensure that we are not allowing our cognitive distortions to harm our students?

THE REFRAME:
WE CAN HACK DEFICIT THINKING

"If, as educators, we don't hold the belief that every
child can learn, what are we even doing?"
— Shannon Williamson

People are more likely to accept information that is consistent with their beliefs. This type of thinking, called *confirmation bias*, focuses on information that reinforces existing ideas. It ignores information that challenges those perceptions. As a result, deficit thinking persists.

Dudley-Marling calls deficit thinking "resilient." The good news is we can hack deficit thinking. We begin by recognizing it, then we consciously implement a new thinking approach. As school psychologist Krista Rice says, this requires one to "[sit] down, like really, truly sitting down, and reflecting on our actions and beliefs. Being ready and willing to be vulnerable to acknowledge the harm we may have caused—and still may be causing."

Part of CBT involves supporting the client in accepting how their thought patterns impact how they feel and behave and how their behaviors impact how they feel and think. Then the therapist assists them in changing those damaged thinking patterns and behaviors. Psychologists believe the "triangle" of thoughts, feelings, and behaviors impact each other equally, so making changes in one area impacts the other two. You can use the concepts of CBT and cognitive distortions to understand the impact of deficit thinking in our classrooms and schools.

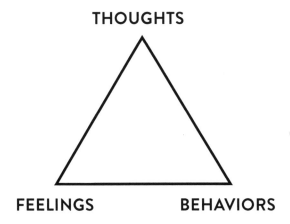

Many people don't realize that they have cognitive distortions or that they operate from a deficit mindset. As Pamela Tucker reiterates, "Often, this thinking is subconscious, and the teacher may not be aware that [they are] guilty of deficit thinking."

However, our student outcomes allow us to reflect on what is truly happening. We created the deficit square (see Image 4.1), which shows how teacher distortions, teacher expectations, teacher behaviors, and student outcomes connect.

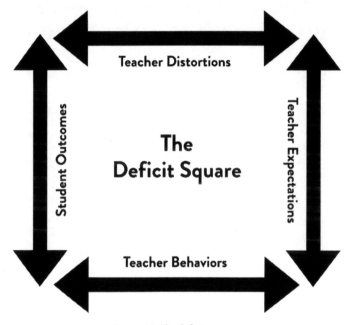

Image 4.1: The deficit square.

You'll notice that the arrow is double-sided to show that all areas impact each other. *When* teachers operate on their deficit distortions, they develop different expectations for student academic outcomes. This leads to different treatment toward students in student groupings, strategies for instruction, feedback received, and learning opportunities offered. These behaviors indirectly communicate our expectations to students and impact student behaviors (student self-concept, motivation and willingness to succeed, and the ability or inability to demonstrate their greatness). All these factors impact outcomes, such as grades and behavior "infractions."

The first step is to identify how to work on our cognitive distortions about students. While researchers have identified general common cognitive distortions, we take these a step further to recognize *deficit distortions*. Deficit distortions, in this case, means wrong and harmful ways of thinking about students. The following deficit distortions are most likely to show up in our education thoughts and practices, specifically when working with Black, Brown, and Indigenous youth and youth with disabilities.

- Commonly termed "black-and-white thinking," *all-or-nothing thinking* views things in absolute terms—situations are either good or bad, and people are either successes or failures. For example, if students continuously make mistakes in their schooling, we may assume they will never be able to succeed.

- *Generalizations* occur when we associate a "rule" with an outcome after one single event, leading us to believe that whenever this single event occurs, the same outcome is inevitable. For example, if we work with a child with a specific difficulty, without success, we may believe that any child with that difficulty will fail. This distortion is incredibly powerful because it can lead us to undermine the impact we can make as educators. It also has serious repercussions for students who have historically been marginalized and are thus prone to be generalized into "one single story."

- *Discounting the positives* involves ignoring or invalidating strengths or positive attributes observed within students. This can occur in many ways. For example, we may hyperfocus on student weaknesses (as our education system has historically encouraged us to do), which leads to us dismissing any traditional or nontraditional strengths a student has that could be tapped into. In another example, we may discount the hard work and effort a student has put into an assignment and instead contribute their success to "luck."

- When you *label* a student, you judge them instead of seeing the behavior as an action that doesn't define them. We may have one negative interaction with a student, and it leads to us labeling them as "a bad kid." This frequently happens with students who have disabilities. People don't view them as a "whole person" but as a person with deficiencies. Labeling can also be triggered when we encounter behaviors from people that confirm implicit stereotypes.

- A *blaming distortion* occurs when we blame our students for situations out of their control. This is incredibly common in schools. It may involve teachers blaming students for any difficulty they present with rather than examining their own teaching practices. It can also involve blaming families for student difficulties observed at school.

By recognizing these cognitive distortions, we can understand how they appear in our classrooms. More specifically, we can recognize how these distortions impact our expectations for students, the ways we interact with students because of these expectations, and how such interactions impact our students.

In Image 4.2, we provide examples of these deficit distortions in action and how they can harm students in observable ways.

ALL OR NOTHING THINKING:
Viewing things in absolute terms–either good or bad; either success or failure

Teacher Distortion	Teacher Expectation	Teacher Behavior
After the first week of school, a teacher feels she has successfully identified all of her "star" students and all of her "struggling" students.	The teacher expects that some of her students will rise to her expectations and others will not.	The teacher challenges her "star" students, provides corrective feedback, and builds them up. The teacher accepts the bare minimum from her "struggling" students and does not provide as much corrective feedback.

Student Outcome

While some students have been afforded rich and rigorous learning opportunities, others have not. Those who have been exposed excel, and those who have not been exposed do not. Potential quantifiable outcomes include lower grades and slower progress for "struggling" students that confirm the "all or nothing" distortion.

OVERGENERALIZATION:
Associating a "rule" with an outcome after one single event

Teacher Distortion	Teacher Expectation	Teacher Behavior
A White teacher working in a predominantly White district had a very difficult time getting ahold of the parent of one of her Black students and has now decided that all Black families do not care about their child's education.	The teacher expects that Black parents do not care about the child's education. If a future Black student struggles (or is being successful!) in class, the teacher does not expect their parent to care.	If a concern is identified in a student's academic or behavior skills, the teacher does not take the time to contact the parent to let them know, as they do not expect to hear back from them.

Student Outcome

Black students are not given the same opportunities of support as White students. Potential quantifiable outcomes are endless.

DISCOUNTING THE POSITIVES:
Ignoring or invalidating strengths or positive attributes observed within students

Teacher Distortion	Teacher Expectation	Teacher Behavior
A student with an IEP has made tremendous progress in meeting their reading goal; however, they are not at grade level yet. The teacher is not fulfilled with this student's progress because of the slow pace they are moving.	The teacher does not expect the student to meet their goal and lowers their expectations for success.	The teacher's interactions with the student are less authentic and congratulatory.
Student Outcome		
The student does not feel as if they are good enough. They start to give up.		

LABELING:
Making entire judgments about students that define them based on one observation

Teacher Distortion	Teacher Expectation	Teacher Behavior
On the first day of school, a student has a difficult time controlling their "shout out" behavior. While on their lunch break, the teacher checks in with their significant other and shares that they've already identified "one problem child."	This child is already expected to be a "problem." Expectations for academic and behavioral success are lowered from the start.	The student is exposed to less positive teacher interactions and more disciplinary interactions.
Student Outcome		
This student does not develop a positive relationship with their teacher or school, leading to disconnectedness and a negative relationship with learning.		

BLAME: Placing blame within our students and families for situations out of their control		
Teacher Distortion	**Teacher Expectation**	**Teacher Behavior**
After introducing a topic and providing an example, a teacher expects his students to have mastered the concept. If some students are still struggling, it is a "them" problem rather than a problem with his approach	Expectations are lowered for all students who cannot grasp the work or who do not connect with this teacher's teaching style.	The teacher appears visibly irritated when students ask for help. Students in turn, stop asking for help.
Student Outcome		
Students do not receive the help or support they need to be successful.		

Image 4.2: Deficit distortions in action.

As Cain states, "[Deficit thinking] creates this lens through which educators look ... That doesn't allow you to see the really important things in students, right? And because of that, because of those blind spots, you begin to fill those blind spots with things that you believe ... And so you take that, and you put it into every single design of lessons or assessments or activities."

Fortunately, CBT impacts our behavior by changing our thinking patterns *and* vice versa. In other words, we need to change our thinking *or* our behavior. This practice works by intentionally creating cognitive dissonance.

Cognitive dissonance happens when someone confronts something that goes against one of their core beliefs. Researchers believe that when two contradictory beliefs are held at the same time ("I thought my Black students were unintelligent, yet they are demonstrating intelligence in front of my eyes"), the individual seeks "resolution."

In short, they change their attitude.

In our case, we seek to create cognitive dissonance via student outcomes that challenge our deficit thoughts. The more opportunities we give our students to prove our deficit distortions wrong, the easier it will be to disrupt those distortions in the first place. This process is mutually and simultaneously beneficial for you and your students.

See Image 4.3 for several ways to hack our deficit distortions about students.

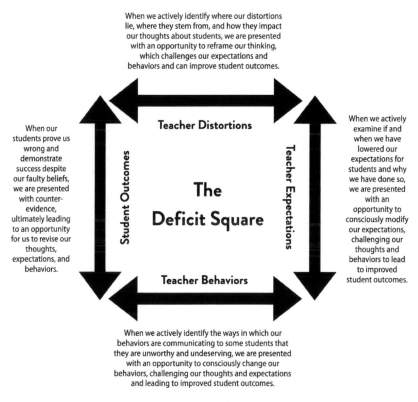

Image 4.3: Hacking your deficit distortions.

We can actively push back against our distorted thoughts by becoming aware of them. Many of our distorted thoughts exist because of the factors to which we attribute misbehavior or learning difficulties. For example, teachers who perceive student misbehavior as intentional or student academic difficulty as "stable" (unable to be changed) are more likely to lower expectations or act less supportive toward such students. Research clearly shows that we are less likely to implement proactive approaches if we perceive our students in this way. However, when we reframe *why* we believe a student behaves in a certain way—our attribution for their behavior—we can disrupt the thought, and that impacts our actions. We are less likely to engage in deficit-based actions when we perceive student misbehavior through a strength-based, unintentional, or growth-based lens.

For example, if a teacher perceives a student as "defiant" because they continuously shout out during teacher-led instruction, the teacher's behaviors will reflect these irritants. However, if we reframe the student's behavior to enthusiasm about the topic, we can maintain high expectations and implement positive behavioral approaches.

This is also where it's important to reflect on our personal contributions. These include the learning environment, our instructional approaches, and other situational factors as potential contributors. As Shannon Williamson says, "Deficit thinking makes it easy for us to stop looking for the best in our students. It's also helpful to flip the

> **We can actively raise our expectations by examining when, where, and why an expectation was lowered for a student or subgroup of students.**

script on deficit language. When I feel my brain blame a student, I immediately force myself to ask, 'What did I do to support this learning?'" The better we can identify how we feel about student actions instead of blaming them, the easier it will be to interrupt deficit-based actions.

We can actively raise our expectations by examining when, where, and why an expectation was lowered for a student or subgroup of students.

Jahsha Tabron, a special education teacher, states, "When we raise our expectations and encourage effort, we reduce stigma and increase student ability."

According to a study conducted by the National Center for Education Statistics (NCES), teachers' expectations impact student success more than a student's own internal motivation! Closing the gap between the expectations we hold and the expectations we aspire to hold is much easier said than done. To do this, we must get vulnerable with ourselves and our students. We need to name our truths, examine how we demonstrate these truths, and be willing to learn how our students perceive and experience these truths. As discussed in Reframe 3, we can gather incredibly helpful information from our students at any time to aid us in better reflecting on our approaches.

Yet, simply holding "high expectations" is not enough if we do not intentionally hold them while reflecting on other aspects of the *deficit square*. We must convince our students that these high expectations are attainable. They must be reachable, realistic, and recognized by our students. We'll tease this apart more in Reframe 6.

Through conscious reflection of our behavioral interactions with students, we can work to enact different practices that challenge our distortions. Cain argues that he has seen the most success when disrupting the "behavior level" in his work. He states,

"I'm not going to attempt to try to change your mind to believe that these kids have strengths. What we're going to do is create these systems and processes that prove these students have strengths. When you see those strengths, your mind is changed, right? You think differently."

The behavior level is all about switching up your actions to allow your students to develop or show you their strengths.

Cain describes another example: "Nearly every school I have had the pleasure to work [at] focused heavily on how parenting affects a student's behavior. Instead of co-creating an environment where both teachers and students could prosper, educators complained about how students missed what they considered [to be] prerequisites to achievement. After interviewing teachers, I compelled them to teach students about said prerequisites. Though it was arduous, I found a few teachers who decided to attempt said strategies. When executed with fidelity, the results were always positive, even if it took time to begin to see results."

This process may include asking your students questions about themselves to counteract some of your previously held beliefs, adapting the way you allow students to express their knowledge, or changing up your instructional techniques. When your behaviors lead to unexpected changes in student behaviors, your thinking patterns can change due to the cognitive dissonance created.

By consciously identifying times when students proved our distortions and expectations wrong, we can disrupt our thinking patterns. The most powerful deterrent to deficit thinking is an observable change in student outcomes—when you observe students engaging in skills that you previously deemed unreachable. As Dudley-Marling states, it is much more difficult to sustain this deficiency narrative when presented with a new narrative that illustrates the abundance of skills that all children possess.

This can occur in many ways but ultimately depends on our observance of students challenging our deficit beliefs, thoughts, and expectations. For example, let's say you have a group of students struggling in your class. After speaking with their teacher from the previous year, you realize that most of your "problem" students were star students last year. The previous student outcomes challenge your current narrative, impacting your thoughts, expectations, and behaviors to better support your students and cultivate those strengths. We must seek out conflicting knowledge.

WHAT YOU CAN DO TOMORROW

"I've had staff I've been working with this year take time to identify their core beliefs by finishing the following statements: 'The purpose of learning is …,' 'Schools are …,' 'The families we serve …,' 'Behavior is …' and then reflect on whether or not our actions (as individuals and in our systems) align with our core beliefs. We like to think we are more justice-minded than our actions show. The first step is to recognize that and come up with a plan for how to align what we do with what we say we believe."

—KRISTA RICE, SCHOOL PSYCHOLOGIST

- **Reflect on your core beliefs using the previous statements.** How have you identified potential cognitive dissonance between what you believe about students and families and what you've learned that your current actions challenge? Or vice versa?

- **Get vulnerable with your students.** Remind students that we're not perfect. When we disclose the distortions we are struggling with, we humanize ourselves and can better form meaningful connections with our students. Ask your students to be vulnerable in return by identifying moments where they perceived something you did as an attack on their self-worth. Reflect on how your students perceive your actions and engage in an open conversation about where the disconnect occurred. This affords you plenty of reflection material and opens the door for accountability on both ends as you seek to disrupt your deficit thinking.

- **Enact the power of "yet."** When you catch yourself blaming students for something out of their control, altering your expectations for certain students, or making assumptions about a student's ability to do something, simply add "yet" to your thoughts. Then actively think about what *you* will do to ensure they move beyond this "yet."

- **Actively alter your language.** The language we use can either perpetuate the distortions in our heads or disrupt them. When we verbalize a distortion, we believe it more. When we verbalize a distortion in the company of others, we communicate that such thinking is appropriate. When we verbalize a distortion in front of our students, they can internalize the belief. Dissect the language you use. What do these words mean? Reflect on why they seem appropriate in a given moment. Consider adopting alternative words.

    Acknowledge your students as human beings

before labels. Language is powerful, and it's a simple way to rewire distorted connections. In Image 4.4, we provide adjectives you can use when thinking about students, talking to coworkers about students, and even talking directly to students.

REFRAMING YOUR ADJECTIVES

Negative Adjective	Positive Adjective
Defiant	Bold/Courageous
Rebellious	Nonconforming
Anti-social	Thoughtful
Hyper/Wild	Energetic
Impatient/Impulsive	Eager
Talkative	Communicative
Restless	Active
Strong-willed	Spirited
Stubborn	Persistent
Emotional	Caring
Dramatic	Expressive
Clingy	Loving
Loud	Expressive
Aggressive	Assertive
Distractible	Interested in the Environment
Sneaky	Creative
Tattletale	Justice-oriented
Disorganized	Spontaneous
Attention-seeker	Connection-seeker
Rigid	Precise

Image 4.4: Reframing your adjectives

A BLUEPRINT FOR FULL IMPLEMENTATION

Step 1: Identify your deficit distortions.

This will be uncomfortable and possibly difficult. Consider identifying your general cognitive distortions. A quick Google search will bring up even more of the most common cognitive distortions. Once you identify those, examine how those cognitive distortions may turn into "deficit distortions" within your classrooms and when working with your students.

Also consider the reasoning assigned to different behaviors. What assumptions do you make about the cause of student needs? Consider the following approach. Think about a student in your class who you feel has been having a difficult time. Now, grab a piece of paper and write down why you think they may be struggling.

- Write down every possible reason that comes to mind.

- Highlight all the times you blamed the student in any way.

- Highlight all the factors within your control in another color.

- Observe which color has taken up most of the space on your paper.

- Identify if there is a pattern that blames students.

Step 2: Reframe your deficit distortions.

This step can involve us actively reframing the behavior we observe within our students and reframing our reasoning for their behaviors. One good way to begin this process is to identify positive characteristics or contributions that the student makes to the learning experience or classroom (see Reframe 6 for more strategies).

This could involve directly reframing the original behavior you identified. For example, rather than "Jamie is always getting into trouble," you could say, "Jamie is very curious about her environment." You could also list Jamie's strengths. If you can't think of any strengths, remember that this says more about your practices than the student. Every child has strengths. It is your job to know them. (See Hack 5 for more about this.)

Step 3: Actively generate counter-thoughts to your beliefs.

Ask yourself, "What if this student proves me wrong?" Or better yet, ask yourself what data you have to support the deficit distortions you have identified. You can also get real with yourself and walk through the scenario of your blame-based attribution to reiterate. Why is it not a beneficial thought? Let's say you attribute a student's misbehavior to them having "not learned how to behave at home."

- Now what?

- How can you better support the student based on this thinking?

- How does it aid you in truly understanding the student?

- How does it make you feel?

Do you feel that you can support this student with your all when you believe that the cause of the behavior is completely out of your control? Is there *nothing* you can control? Now that you've walked through that train of thought, ask yourself what else could be occurring or other ways you could consider the situation.

Another simple (and often forgotten) way to reframe the distortions we've developed is to simply ask our students *why* they're doing what they're doing. Nine times out of ten, they will tell us a reason we hadn't yet considered that can reframe our thinking.

Step 4: Examine your expectations.

Ask yourself what expectations you *aspire* to hold for all students. Next, reflect on the expectations you currently hold. This is easier said than done and requires intentionality and vulnerability. While no teacher wants to admit that they have lowered their expectations for some students, we need to forget our pride and acknowledge our true actions. Importantly, while we want to hold high expectations, they may not look the same for all students. The last thing we want to do is set students up for failure by creating unrealistic and unreachable expectations. So, the question becomes, "What are challenging but attainable and reachable goals that each student will reach or exceed?" There are many ways to do this *with* your students.

Consider setting identifiable expectations at the beginning of the year with each student and allow for opportunities to review and revise them throughout the year. These can be behavioral or academic expectations, but they must be attainable and agreed upon by your students. Encourage your students to share their expectations with the class. Develop an accountability plan that outlines how the students or you will respond when someone forgets about these expectations. This normalizes to students that they all have different goals, which is okay! It allows your students to be involved in setting high expectations for themselves, and it holds everyone accountable for maintaining these expectations. By reviewing them throughout the year, you can reimagine the students' relationships with the idea of "failure." You can normalize the act of adjusting your goals or expectations, as needed, for yourself. However, it is up to you to continuously challenge your students and remind them that they can meet their goals.

Step 5: Create opportunities for your students to meet or exceed your expectations.

We can do this by truly *knowing* our students and seeing them for who they are. When we understand our students' strengths, we can better create the environments they need to display their strengths. We must be open-minded in our approaches and allow our students to take the reins when possible. For example, when we allow our students to lead a lesson, we may be surprised by their method of thinking about a topic. When we cultivate that natural curiosity, we set up our students to exceed our expectations.

It is also important to provide clear expectations about success criteria. Don't assume that students already know it. Give them a rubric. Sure, we mostly dedicate rubrics to college and not elementary or secondary school, but why aren't we more clear about what we want our students to show us? When we give examples, we actively encourage our students to produce what we expect from them. We must also provide actionable feedback and opportunities for revision. There is no reason why a student should be allowed to complete low-quality work without reflection and revision expectations. Encourage students to come to you for help and ensure they know that while you expect them to achieve, you will also support them.

Step 6: Involve your students and encourage them to hold you accountable.

We've already discussed how student voices are often missing in conversations about teaching practices. When we don't ask our students how they are feeling, we make assumptions about how they are feeling. We can strive to understand our students' worlds as they see them and to understand how they perceive our expectations and actions. We can honor them rather than dismiss them.

When we cultivate spaces for natural accountability, we cultivate community. That is incredibly powerful in disrupting the perception of deficits.

OVERCOMING PUSHBACK

Because deficit distortions are the norm in schools, you will face pushback within yourself and others as you work to disrupt them. Deficit thinking is so powerful because it is easy to succumb to these pushbacks. Here are a few common types of concerns and how to address them.

I'm struggling to come up with attributions that are within my control. Fear not: we have a simple strategy to reframe any attribution to be within our control. Begin every attribution with: "I/we need to support the student." This requires you to come up with areas that you have control over. This can be as simple as reframing. "He doesn't know how to control his emotions" changes to "We need to support the student in learning how to control his emotions." And from here, you are already thinking about the student differently. You are not reducing him to a deficit; you are considering how you can make a difference. You remember that this behavior is changeable, and you can assist in changing it.

I don't know how to respond to others engaging in deficit thinking. It can be uncomfortable to be in a space where your coworkers or teams frequently verbalize negative beliefs or assumptions about students. We offer the following potential responses to keep in your back pocket:

1. What makes you think that?

2. Have you asked the student about this?

3. Have you asked the parents about this?

4. That isn't under our control. Can you think of anything we *do* have control over?

5. I understand that students spend most of their time at home, and their parents heavily influence them, but blaming their behaviors on that isn't helping.

6. I used to think like that about students. I've found that it makes me feel more in control when I think about it like this: _____.

7. What's another way of thinking about this?

8. What changes can we make at the school level to better support this student?

9. What can I do to help you support this child?

10. I've recently learned about deficit thinking and my responsibility to change my thought patterns. It really helped me! Would you be interested in learning about it?

I'm struggling to connect my thoughts to my behaviors. It's tough to make this connection, especially when it involves what we do for a living. Start by actively examining your thinking and behavior patterns. Relate those to your feelings to aid in thinking critically about your actions. For example, we have all come to work in a bad mood for whatever reason—maybe we didn't get enough sleep, maybe we're running late, maybe we spilled our coffee on the way into the building. Consider mapping out the deficit square we provided, or create your own. Fill in some different emotions you have started the school day with, along with how those feelings could impact your interactions with students. After you understand how basic emotions can impact you, get vulnerable with yourself. Then you're open to reflecting on any deficit distortions that could also impact your behaviors.

THE REFRAME IN ACTION

A third grade teacher, Ms. Thomas, recently learned about deficit thinking and works to reframe her assumptions about her students. As a White woman, she is familiar with the concepts of implicit bias and systemic racism and looks for opportunities to reflect on her participation in this system. She has found the deficit distortions framework particularly interesting, especially as she seeks to ensure that her classroom is equitable and reflects her values. She especially resonated with the "blame" distortion.

After some uncomfortable reflection, she realized she placed inherent blame on her Black students. She recognized that it was unintentional but took ownership over the impact she had on previous Black students. She takes the time to calculate the risk of her Black students receiving poorer grades and more office referrals than White students. She found serious discrepancies and began to reflect on why she was more likely to blame her Black students for difficulties they faced. She challenged herself to think about previous students with behavioral needs and what attributions she made for those challenges.

One example comes to mind from the previous school year. It involves a White student named Jack and a Black student named Michael. Upon reflection, she realized that their behaviors were similar. However, she could get ahold of Jack's parents fairly easily. They always answered the phone and were extremely cooperative and responsive. On the other hand, she thinks she can count on one hand the number of times she was able to successfully speak with Michael's mother. She recalls speaking of this with Michael's other teachers and remembers everyone making assumptions about Michael's mother—saying that she was a single mom with a revolving door of men coming in and out of her life. They assumed she didn't care about Michael.

Thomas recalls giving up on attempting to reach her. In this example, she realized that her assumptions about Michael's mother being a single Black mother and not caring about her son led to her lowering her expectations for Michael's behavioral success. This led to a change in her behaviors—namely, attempting to gain his mother's perspective and to brainstorm success strategies. Michael's behavior went mostly unaddressed for the rest of the year, and the school suspended him toward the end of it. Thomas wonders if anything would have been different if she had not allowed her blaming thoughts to impact how she approached Michael.

She challenged herself to think of any other times she may have allowed her expectations to fall because of assumptions made about a child's family. She immediately thought of a current student—Brandon. Brandon reminded her of Michael in some ways—and she caught her deficit belief in action, challenging herself to not overgeneralize the needs of her Black male students. Brandon also demonstrated challenging behaviors, and it wasn't easy to get ahold of Brandon's parents.

Instead of talking about Brandon in the teacher's lounge with the third grade team, where the team reinforced deficiencies and blame, Thomas asked Brandon about his family. She asked him what he thought would be the best way to get ahold of his parents if needed. He shared that his dad worked the night shift and his mom was busy with his younger brother and pregnant with his baby sister. This new information reframed some of Thomas's beliefs about Brandon's needs, as she realized how busy his family was.

Thomas decided to send a note home with Brandon and encouraged him to be her secret messenger to get the note to his parents.

Brandon's mother emailed Ms. Thomas the next day and shared that she had been having issues with her cell phone lately and hadn't received any phone calls. She said that email was the preferred contact method until she fixed her phone.

They eventually had a conversation about Brandon's behaviors, and Ms. Thomas learned that Brandon's grandfather had recently passed away. Brandon was very close to his grandfather, and his mother thought that some of his behaviors were related to this loss. Thomas decided to involve the school counselor to support Brandon. Eight weeks later, Brandon was a whole new child. While it was a long process, Thomas now had a clear example to rely on that showed her the power of reframing her thoughts, expectations, and behaviors to better serve her students.

Deficit distortions will often not be as clear-cut to identify and address. It takes true reflection and courage to try something new. We challenge you to push through the discomfort and see what happens when you give your students and their families a chance to show you the *why* behind their actions.

BUILD ON STUDENT STRENGTHS
From What's Wrong to What's Strong

Well-being should be taught in school because it would be an antidote to the runaway incidence of depression, a way to increase life satisfaction, and an aid to better learning and more creative thinking.

— MARTIN SELIGMAN, FOUNDER OF POSITIVE PSYCHOLOGY

THE BELIEF:
WE SHOULD ONLY FOCUS ON ADDRESSING STUDENT DEFICIENCIES

WE RECENTLY HELD a workshop to help educators name, know, and use their strengths. We asked the audience to raise their hands if they could readily name their top five strengths. Out of about 250 participants, only about fifteen people raised their hands. We then asked how many people could name two or three of their top strengths. This time, about ten to fifteen more hands went up. Then, we asked how many people could name at least a single strength they might have. Still, only a few more hands went up.

In this exercise, the intent is to see how many people can readily name their top strengths. Like clockwork, regardless of the city, location, or demographic, few people can readily name their strengths. But why? Why do people have such a hard time identifying and naming their top strengths?

For starters, it's hard for people to speak affirmatively about themselves. Sadly, they have been conditioned or taught that their weaknesses define them. As a result, they view and maneuver the world through a deficit lens. Another reason people struggle is that it's much easier to name our weaknesses and deficits. This difficulty isn't exclusive to adults either.

As practitioners inside schools, we have found that students across age and grade levels struggle to identify and name their strengths. It's not surprising that a room full of 250 adults struggled to name their strengths. They once were children who, most likely, were never required to readily name, know, and use their strengths. Our responsibility as educators is to help students leverage their assets in a way that no one taught us.

THE REFRAME:
BUILD UP STUDENT STRENGTHS

Students need to be able to name, know, and use their strengths. Educators can be much more intentional about helping students build their strengths, not just prioritizing their weaknesses and what they can't do. School administrators, mental health personnel, teachers, and other school-based staff must commit to using a strength-based approach to help students actively develop their strengths.

Benefits of a strength-based approach to building up students

The strength-based approach focuses on a person's unique strengths, assets, and capabilities. It is a philosophy that sees people as resourceful, resilient, and capable of change. This approach empowers people to take control of their lives and create positive outcomes for themselves.

We emphasize the key belief that every person has many strengths and abilities they use when facing challenges. We offer a solution-focused perspective with clients to identify their strengths and utilize them to overcome problems in their lives.

The strength-based approach values building off what works rather than focusing on what doesn't. It promotes a positive view of the individual and encourages connecting with one's social supports like family or community to spur on their transformation.

We must promote individual well-being. It's holistic and human-centered because it sees the humanity in people. In the context of schools, using a strength-based approach allows every student the potential to thrive. Students not only learn to understand their strengths within this system, but they also use them in the context of their lives and communities. The motivation is simple: it works. Research shows that when students understand their strengths and use them to gain skills and increase productivity, they experience stronger self-confidence, greater academic success, and better relationships with peers, teachers, and parents.

When we encourage children to identify, explore, and use their strengths, they gain the confidence to develop skills in other areas.

Many young people experience feelings of inadequacy and self-doubt as they try to thrive in a world that doesn't always see their gifts and talents as important. By encouraging students to understand their innate skills and abilities, you can help them remember how exceptional they are.

As an educator (or parent), to help students develop their strengths, place value on what's working over what's not working. To help people find value in what's working, ask questions like:

- What makes you feel happy?

- What draws people to you?

- What activities are easy for you?

- What do you consider to be your greatest strengths?

- Describe a time when things went well for you. Why did they go well?

When a child understands their strengths, it equips them to make better choices about how to spend their time—and how to shape their lives. When we encourage children to identify, explore, and use their strengths, they gain the confidence to develop skills in other areas. Research from the University of Pennsylvania and the field of Positive Psychology demonstrates that helping students build their strengths promotes academic achievement, happiness, and a sense of self-efficacy. It supports student well-being.

Perhaps the most important aspect of helping students develop strengths is teaching them how to be solution-focused. This can be difficult for students because it involves teaching them to focus on what worked in the past and what works now, even when facing insurmountable problems or obstacles.

One effective way to teach this skill is to have students keep a journal to write down each day's successes. You can do this as a class, small group, or at the individual level. Everyone can share something they've done well or accomplished that day. You can also create a class journal where each student contributes one entry per week. Parents or caregivers can do this at home too.

One of our favorite activities helps students build their strengths by noticing and reflecting on what went well. The activity is called Three Good Things. Dr. Martin Seligman and his team at the University of Pennsylvania studied and researched this activity, which increases happiness and decreases depressive symptoms for six months. Participants in the Three Good Things exercise showed beneficial effects one month following the test.

At the one-month follow-up, participants were happier and less depressed than they had been at the baseline, and they stayed happier and less depressed at the three-month and six-month follow-ups.

This is a powerful exercise because it shifts your focus from things that were wrong to things that were strong. This positive mindset can improve your overall well-being and lift your mood. The Three Good Things exercise helps students reflect on themselves—*and* why they were good. See Image 5.1.

Try this exercise with your students or loved ones at home:

1. At the end of each day, write down Three Good Things that happened that day.

2. Write *why* each thing went well.

3. Do this for at least a week straight.

Image 5.1: The Three Good Things activity.

WHAT YOU CAN DO TOMORROW

By taking a strength-based approach to education, you can help your students develop their skills and talents to realize their full potential. Let's help kids figure out what they're good at and improve those areas. Let's prioritize helping students build their strengths and practice using them daily. That will help them feel happier, experience more flow, and keep doing activities they enjoy—even when they have to do other activities they don't like. Educators and even parents who use a strength-based approach will help children become more invested in their learning and more engaged in the classroom.

The SPOT process can help students develop their strengths. It stands for Strength observation; Progress over perfection; Opportunity to shine; and Teach, try, and tap into strengths.

Strength observation. A strength observation is a way to proactively search for strengths in your students. Try immersing yourself in their environment, such as the classroom, hallway, cafeteria, and after-school events. A strength observation differs from a traditional observation because you are intentionally searching for the positive. As a strength observer, it's not your job to be right but to learn more about who you observe. That requires being open and receptive to what you may or may not see.

What is the most important trait in a strength observer? Curiosity! You need to understand your students' behaviors, experiences, and desires. You'll need to ask questions that you might think are obvious or irrelevant. The more time you spend with them, the more you learn about their strengths. One of the most important steps to becoming a strength observer is adopting an explorer's mindset. This means that you approach the observation with an open mind—without any preconceived notions—and seek to discover various strengths. It also means being open to every possibility. When you immerse yourself in your students' worlds, you give yourself permission to be curious and wonder. Then you open yourself to discovering new strengths within your students.

In a successful strength observation, you will ask questions, expect unconventional answers, and learn about the students' worlds. Searching for strengths in your students might seem intuitive, but it's not. Since most of us, as educators, were trained to identify students' deficits, we have to actively work to identify their strengths. Pay attention to the following:

- Does the student work better independently or in a group?
- When does the student show excitement, boredom, more energy or less energy, frustration, or sustained focus?
- How easily do they initiate tasks, shift between tasks, and stay on task?
- Are they inspiring or motivating others?
- Are they creative in how they approach a given task?
- Do they leverage resources or social capital in a meaningful way?

- What was challenging for the student?
- What seemed easy for the student?
- What patterns did you notice throughout the observation?

After the observation, review your findings with the student. Specifically, share the strengths you identified. For example, if you observed a student during math class while they had to sustain attention over a long period of time, you might say, "Your attention to detail is strong, and you were able to focus on the entire task to get the job done." Maybe you observed a student who didn't contribute much during the brainstorming portion of the group activity in social studies. Still, that student captivated his peers and had them on the edge of their seats during the group presentation to the whole class.

Next, have the student offer their reflections on how they view their strengths. Ask them if they agree with your assessment. This is an opportunity to get feedback on how well your observations match up with how the students see themselves—and it also helps students learn more about themselves!

To take this a step further, help students reflect on their strengths by asking questions like:

- What do you think you are good at?
- What do you love to do?
- What comes easily to you?
- Are there any activities that make you lose track of time?

Progress over perfection. Identifying and using strengths can be hard because most of us aren't used to tapping into our strengths. The key here is to help young people understand the importance of progress. The reality is that routinely using your strengths is a skill. LeBron James is arguably the greatest basketball player of our generation, and he practices his craft daily.

We can also practice our strength-finding skills every day. Some days will be more challenging than others. Make progress toward the goal, not perfection. Help your students find new ways to use their strengths and get better every day.

Opportunity to shine. When students use their strengths, it gives them a chance to shine, and they are more likely to experience success. This builds self-efficacy and gives them a reason to persist, even when tasks are challenging.

Simply put, when students have an opportunity to use their strengths and shine, they experience positive emotions and feel good about themselves.

Imagine a child with perseverance as a strength who only has one shot at succeeding at a task. If they aren't successful on the first try, that child might become frustrated and learn that you have to be perfect, contributing to anxiety. Imagine if a student has a signature strength of perseverance, and you give them multiple chances to demonstrate mastery. The student might not succeed on the first try, the second try, or even the third. But providing a student who demonstrates perseverance with the opportunity to work at the task until they are successful will help them feel accomplished and continue to work at it even when they face adversity.

Creating opportunities for students to use and demonstrate their strengths is an excellent way to build self-confidence. Students will begin to believe in themselves, realize they are capable, and leverage their strengths in meaningful ways. Also, there is value in helping students recognize and identify missed opportunities for using their strengths. The idea here is that if students can identify these missed opportunities, then it might help to increase their awareness of future opportunities to use strengths.

Teach, try, and tap into strengths. Teach students to explicitly name their strengths. Help them to build up their strength-based vocabulary, and show them the power of "yet." Instead of a student saying they are not good at math facts, please encourage them to say, "I might not be the best in math facts—*YET.*" Encourage young people to *try* their strengths in new ways. If their strength is "focus," ask them to try a new task like finding a solution to a problem no one has figured out yet.

Help your students find ways to tap into the strengths of others. Why? Because the best schools, communities, teams, and organizations know how to harness the strengths of each other—and you can help your students do the same.

This means helping students become well-attuned to their strengths and limitations and learn how to work with others with different strengths and limitations.

For example, some people are fantastic at making decisions quickly and effectively. Others are great at seeing all possible consequences of a decision. Some find inspiration in unexpected places. When you have a team that is familiar with each individual's approach, you can create a culture where everyone feels comfortable contributing to what they're best at. This leads to bigger and better ideas than if everyone just worked on their own, and it also leads to increased trust in the team—which is what makes them stronger overall.

One way to help people tap into the strengths of others is to ask them, "How might you use one of your strengths to help someone else?"

A BLUEPRINT FOR FULL IMPLEMENTATION

Now that you've learned how to SPOT your students' strengths, let's focus on helping young people name and identify their top strengths. In this blueprint, we get a little more granular and explicit. Here's a winning blueprint you can use to help you get started on building your students' strengths.

Step 1: Pick an assessment.

You can use various assessments for youth to help them name their strengths. This is a great first step. Use strength-based assessments or surveys to help you accurately identify them in students. Here are a few to get you started:

- **CliftonStrengths for Students.** Formerly StrengthsQuest, this test helps students discover their strengths and learn what's unique about them. The program uses Gallup's world-renowned CliftonStrengths assessment to measure thirty-four research-validated talent themes. It's designed for children aged ten to fourteen and gives them the chance to discover their talents at an early age. It then teaches students how to develop their talents into strengths—and, ultimately, how to be happier and more successful.

- **Values in Action (VIA) Survey of Character Strengths.** The VIA Survey of Character Strengths is a 240-item self-report questionnaire intended for adult use. It connects to the twenty-four strengths of character that comprise the VIA Classification. We like the VIA assessments not just because we value the work of Martin Seligman and Chris Peterson but also because they have done the research to develop strength-based assessments for youth.

- **VIA Youth Survey.** A new and improved version of the VIA Youth Survey launched in October 2021, and it contains revisions to all twenty-four scales. The VIA Institute recommends this as the preferred measure of character strengths in youth. Extensive research backs up these scales and even creates surveys for younger students. The VIA has surveys for youth ages eight to twelve and thirteen to seventeen.

- **The Character Strengths Inventory for Children (CSI-C) Ages Seven to Twelve.** The CSI-C is a self-report character inventory for children that was written for easy administration directly to elementary students. It uses developmental and age-appropriate items from over a two-year period, based on commentary from clinical and developmental psychologists, teachers, and feedback from focus groups of parents and children. Data supports the validity of the inventory.

- **The Character Strengths Inventory for Early Childhood (CSI-EC).** Developed by professor Anat Shoshani, this inventory measures a young child's character strengths. This ninety-six-item questionnaire consists of statements about a child's behavior, and parents indicate how true each statement is using a five-point scale from 1 (not at all true) to 5 (very true). It measures twenty-four character strengths.

- **Behavioral and Emotional Rating Scale, Third Edition (BERS-3).** This strength-based assessment system measures behavior from the perspectives of the student, parent, and teacher. Counselors use it to evaluate students for pre-referral services and placement for specialized services and to measure the outcomes of services. The BERS-3 identifies students' behavior and emotional strengths and the areas to improve education.

While this list of strength-based assessments is not exhaustive, it's a good start to using well-researched and validated assessments to help your students identify and name their strengths. Once you've selected the most appropriate assessment, create time and space for your students to take the assessment.

Step 2: Set the time to assess.

Once you pick an assessment, set the appropriate time for your students to take the test. Depending on the assessment, it may take anywhere from fifteen minutes to forty-five minutes per child. Be sure to consider the assessment length while picking the best assessment. Ideally, your school administration will set aside plenty of time for your students to take it. If needed, seek help from the school counselor or psychologist. One might even consider having all students complete the assessment at the beginning of the year to guide classroom practices.

Step 3: Review results.

This is an important step. Reviewing the assessment results *with* your students is important for several reasons. First, some students might be unaware that they *have* strengths. This is a moment to deliberately hype them up. Second, it's also a moment to explain their strengths to them.

Step 4: Make it plain.

After reviewing the results with your students, ask them to list their top strengths. This will help them remember their strengths, and they can refer back to them as needed. It also reinforces the fact that they *have* strengths.

Step 5: Practice. Practice. Practice.

As discussed earlier in this Reframe, allow students to use their strengths as often as possible. If a student has the strength of a relator, allow that student to work in groups and collaboratively with others. If a student has the strength of strategy, allow them to take the lead by coming up with a plan to help their group accomplish a task. If a student has the strength of forming ideas and concepts, allow them time and space to develop ideas for a project they might be working on. The key takeaway is to provide young people with opportunities to put their strengths into action. The more they practice putting their strengths into action, the more comfortably they will use them.

Step 6: Reflect.

Reflecting on strengths is a great way to improve your strengths; reflections help you note what's working, what's not working, and what you can improve. Here are reflective questions your students can use:

- Name a time when you used your strengths.
- How did it feel when you used your strengths?
- How can you use your strengths to help a friend?
- Name a way you can use your strengths more often.
- What gives you energy?
- What comes easy for you that others might find difficult?
- What's stopping you from using your strengths?

Step 7: Hold check-ins.

You might find it beneficial to have weekly, bi-weekly, monthly, or even quarterly check-ins with your students. During the check-ins, you can review the strengths of each student. Intentional check-ins can be powerful and meaningful when you use reflective questions with students. It helps them continuously cultivate their strengths and ask questions to further their understanding. Finally, checking in with students will help you discover any barriers that might be preventing students from empowering themselves.

OVERCOMING PUSHBACK

It won't be easy to shift from what's wrong to what's strong. Here are a few common types of concerns for this Reframe and how to address them.

You shouldn't prioritize strengths over weaknesses. It's true that we shouldn't ignore areas of weakness, but just because we ignore them doesn't mean they will go away. Ignoring areas of weakness might cause more harm. The problem, however, is when we ignore strengths. A more balanced approach involves acknowledging areas of improvement and leveraging strengths.

Focusing on strengths is toxic positivity. A strength-based approach doesn't mean practicing toxic positivity or adopting an everything-is-fine approach to life that rejects difficult emotions in favor of a cheerful—often falsely positive—facade. Positivity becomes toxic when it masks true feelings and we act as though everything is fine when it isn't. It's a fake way to make people feel better when they feel bad—but the problem is when it's not genuine. Instead, we can help students SPOT their strengths, practice progress over perfection, and learn how to effectively deal with adversity because it's a natural part of life.

Not everyone has a strength. This simply is not true. When someone implies that they don't have any strengths or a student or colleague doesn't have any strengths, you must reject that sentiment. This type of statement is rooted in deficit ideology. To shift away from comments such as these, we must help people understand the potential of every person. As educators, parents, and caregivers, you must commit to seeing the potential in everyone. Now that you know how to SPOT strengths, you can work with others to help them SPOT strengths in themselves and in their students.

THE REFRAME IN ACTION

Sheree is a student who had a reputation for fighting, not getting along with peers, engaging in inappropriate behaviors under typical circumstances, and having difficulty regulating her emotions. Her teachers were frustrated and didn't know what to do. They referred her for an evaluation to determine whether she had an emotional disability, and the school psychologist conducted a classroom observation to see what was happening.

The psychologist observed Sheree in her geometry class. Sheree sat at a desk with her peers with her head down during the observation. Her teacher gave instructions and then passed out an assignment for students to work on. The teacher gave Sheree a paper and told her to sit up and get started. Sheree ignored her teacher. The teacher whispered to the psychologist, "She does this every day and won't do any work."

The psychologist observed Sheree sitting with her head down for about five minutes but noticed her hand moving. The psychologist discreetly moved a little closer to get a better look at what Sheree was doing, and it was mind-blowing. She was doodling 3D geometric shapes that appeared to pop off the page and into the room. It was an immaculate drawing and rendering. The psychologist looked around to see if anyone else noticed the same thing: no one had ever talked about her drawing ability, creating these 3D renderings, or her potential. The psychologist broke observation procedures and asked Sheree what she was working on.

Sheree said, "Oh, nothing. I'm just bored."

Sheree had worked with the psychologist, so they had a good relationship. She said, "I know, I have to do my work. I'm just bored." The psychologist told her that he cared about the work but was more impressed with the drawing and asked a silly question.

"You know how to draw?"

She said, "Yeah, but no one ever asked."

That blew the psychologist away. Standing there puzzled and confused because he had only heard negative things about this student, he asked Sheree if she knew how to do the assignment the teacher gave.

She responded, "That work is too easy for me."

The psychologist replied, "If it's easy, how come you never do it."

Sheree laughed and said, "Because it's dumb."

The psychologist, *curious and intrigued*, then challenged Sheree. "Okay, then do it."

She sat up, and in three minutes and thirty seconds, she completed the entire assignment.

"Done," Sheree replied. She put her head down in the coolest manner and went back to doodling.

The psychologist stood there in awe.

What happens when we fail to recognize the brilliance our students already have? What happens when we recognize the untapped potential of our students?

The psychologist completed a comprehensive psychological evaluation, including behavior rating scales, cognitive functioning, academic skills, and parent input. You name it, the psychologist did it. Perhaps the most valuable part was talking with the student about her strengths, talking with her mom about her strengths, and seeing her potential. At the review meeting, the psychologist reviewed the results of the evaluation. Sheree had scored through the roof on her cognitive assessment, especially in the areas of fluid reasoning on her IQ test. Fluid reasoning measures a person's ability to understand underlying conceptual relationships among visual objects, use reasoning, apply rules, understand quantitative reasoning, and express abstract thinking. Sheree had scored the highest the psychologist had ever seen in ten years of conducting psychological evaluations. Sheree was gifted, and no one had noticed. At this point, Sheree was a sophomore in high school. How does a student who is in the top 99th percentile go unnoticed for years?

Deficit thinking.

The psychologist highlighted the many strengths of Sheree during the individualized education program (IEP) meeting and showed the team what was possible. Sheree's mom was in tears because she had never heard the amazing things her daughter was capable of; she had only heard the negatives. The psychologist recommended that Sheree not be identified as a student with an emotional disability and instead challenged the team to leverage her strengths. He suggested placing Sheree in AP and honor classes to challenge her with teachers who would support her—but push her as well.

The psychologist worked with her teachers to be collaborative in providing solutions and strategies from a strength-based approach. He also recommended behavioral support to address the challenges of getting along with peers and her emotional dysregulation.

This is an example of how we can balance our approach through a strength-based lens. We don't ignore weaknesses. Instead, we must approach this work with a healthy sense of curiosity and intrigue to notice the untapped potential of young people. By doing so, we can unlock the brilliance within them.

We believe that all children have strengths, and as educators, teachers, and parents, we can best respond to children based on those strengths. If a child doesn't demonstrate a strength we recognize in them, it doesn't mean the child has a deficit or is somehow lacking. Instead, it means the child needs our help to communicate or show their strengths so we can understand and assist them. We also know that education, mental health, and social service treatment plans can improve their focus on strengths. We all need to work together to help people understand their strengths and find ways to use them.

DIFFERENCES ARE STRENGTHS
Abling the Environment

I believe the neurodiversity community and social model of medicine [are] trying to move our field, and the medical field, into a model where we look at difference[s] as the natural experience of human existence and think about the environments that cause the deficits, not the child or the person.

— DANIELLE CHRISTY, EDUCATIONAL PSYCHOLOGIST

THE BELIEF:
DISABILITIES REPRESENT DEFICITS

HISTORICALLY AND PRESENTLY, our schools define "normal" as those who are worthy of receiving a rigorous education. Schools often don't welcome those who don't fit into this box. But what about special education, you ask? Wasn't special education designed for this very purpose—to ensure that all students, regardless of their physical, mental, and academic abilities, are provided a free and appropriate education?

To answer this question, we must first remember that our schools were historically and traditionally organized to accommodate a narrow range of human differences. This positioned students for failure if they didn't fit this mold, especially students identified as having a disability.

As we've previously mentioned, "special education" has traditionally aimed to identify an academic, behavioral, cognitive, social-emotional, or adaptive "deficit" that is *intrinsic* to the individual. It makes a student eligible for services designed to "fix" that deficit. We identify deficits by comparing students' skills to their same-age peers. As Dr. Tim Runge says, "That is, does this kid have deficiencies that are so deviant or disparate from typical that they need to be in a different school? ... Does this kid need special classrooms and services because they've got some deficit that is internal to them?"

Consider this scenario described by Danielle Christy, educational psychologist: "All of us as educators should think about how much we would like it if we had a meeting for ourselves every year with a bunch of people at a table to talk about our deficits. And then we got to talk about all the goals we didn't meet and get more assessments done to highlight all the things we struggle with. How many of us would want to go to that meeting?"

After all, teachers often walk out of an evaluation with a single administrator feeling the same way; imagine three to five administrators, each tasked with identifying a different area of deficit within your teaching practices.

So, what's wrong with viewing disabilities as deficits? It minimizes the student to one label.

- "They're SPED (special education)."

- "They're tier three."

- "They're in my red group."

- "They're an intervention student."

This thinking magnifies deficit and minimizes strength. How many individualized education programs (IEPs) spend just as much time identifying student strengths as capturing student deficits?

When we fail to focus on strengths, the outcomes are extraordinarily negative—a lowering of expectations, a watering down of the curriculum, and a harmful cycle that sets up students for failure.

Runge continues, "Many times, a deficit thinking approach leads to very few, if any, interventions or ways to try to assist the individual because they have a problem that's internal to them and we can't fix it."

Our current way of identifying, placing, and supporting students with identified disabilities serves as another mechanism to find fault within our students. It does not emphasize that our practices often cause the disabling. Our whole special education system is rooted in deficit thinking.

We want to share the story of Rashad Bilal, co-host of the "biggest show ever," *Earn Your Leisure*. Rashad disrupted the financial industry and made financial literacy responsive and culturally relevant to people who have been historically marginalized.

In his TED Talk, Rashad highlighted how school taught him everything except what was important. He explained how his school diagnosed him with a learning disability and recommended an IEP. Although his teachers thought he couldn't learn, Rashad simply felt disinterested in what they taught. In so many ways, Rashad's story is the story of young people across our nation. Instead of addressing issues with the antiquated way we teach children, educators focus on deficiencies within children.

Rashad talks about his mother, a teacher who fought for him to remain in the general education classroom setting. He then poses an important question, "What if I didn't have a mother who was knowledgeable enough to fight for my education?" He explains how many students don't have parents who understand the IEP process.

Rashad asks how labeling children might psychologically harm them in certain instances. He says that our traditional approach could ruin the rest of their young lives because they go on to think that they are not able to learn or achieve at high levels. This is how deficit thinking shows up.

While Rashad might have had differing abilities or been disinterested in school, the default function was to remediate his deficiencies. By identifying the worst in Rashad and seeking to "solve" his academic problems, the default model tells us to refer, assess, and place the student in special education. Focusing solely on remediating student deficiencies leads to instructional practices that diminish student learning. It limits access to the rich learning opportunities routinely afforded to students in affluent, high-achieving schools and classrooms. Students targeted by these practices learn less because of the scope and pace of the remedial curricula.

Rashad's mother fought against his placement in a self-contained classroom because, as an educator, she understood that it wasn't the answer. She saw something in her child that educators couldn't see for some reason. She saw his potential, and she was right.

Rashad became a highly sought-after financial advisor on Park Avenue, where he noticed a major gap while working with the wealthy and elite. He noticed that the financial world consisted of "eighty-year-old White men, which didn't reflect me," as Rashad emphatically stated in his talk. Here's the thing: the lack of representation in the financial industry on Park Avenue, his educational experiences, and being incorrectly labeled and placed in special education made him self-conscious. Despite his insecurities and doubts, Rashad disrupted the financial literacy world through his platform and completely revolutionized how people understand finances. So, if Rashad demonstrates this level of success after graduating, how could he have been disabled?

Disabilities only exist in contexts or environments that lead to disabling. For example, when someone is in a wheelchair, they are only "disabled" if our spaces expect that everyone walks. If stairs are the only method of navigating the space, the environment and expectations have disabled the person in the wheelchair by assuming anything "different" is a "personal deficit." On the other hand, if the space expects a range of physical differences and allows multiple ways to navigate the space, we no longer disable people.

Let's also look at the in-between of these examples. Suppose our spaces expect that most people will be able to walk and a few may not. In that case, we may believe that providing a small, hidden accommodation for those in a wheelchair (an elevator at the far end of the space or a ramp with a separate entrance) will suffice. But this method continues to disable people by making their differences a known burden.

As Dudley-Marling states, students can't be "learning disabled" on their own. The presence of a learning disability requires the specific actions of people (like students, teachers, and related service providers) engaging in the right behaviors at exactly the right times. When we think of it in this way, we can acknowledge that learning disabilities don't exist solely within the minds and bodies of individual students. They're created in the interactions and dynamics between students, staff, curricula, and classrooms.

Let's go back to Rashad. His school almost placed him into special education. He would have received a watered-down version of the curriculum, further disengaging him since he was already disinterested in school—and further leading him to blame himself. In other instances, our special education system reinforces weaknesses by solely focusing on those weaknesses—and at a pace that further separates students from their peers.

- How do we ensure that our environments accept differences without disabling anyone?

- What would special education look like without this emphasis on deficits?

- Is there a way to acknowledge human differences without disabling our students?

- Can we ensure that students with differences are adequately supported and continue to receive rigorous instruction without being singled out and separated?

The answer is yes. And it begins with a movement away from the deficit model. The most powerful part of Rashad's talk was when he said, "What I thought was crippling me was actually my superpower."

How can we help young people identify their superpowers? Our jobs as educators, parents, and leaders should not solely be to identify deficits, deficiencies, and problems. Our job and mission must be to amplify the strengths of children (and staff) to lead satisfying, fulfilling, and meaningful lives.

> We wouldn't need special education if we didn't confine the educational experience to one approach and method and expect similar outcomes.

THE REFRAME:
DIFFERENCES ARE STRENGTHS

Imagine an educational system without special education, norm-based comparisons, or averages. In a world where requiring different levels of support isn't negative, Rashad and his mother would have been less traumatized.

An ideal educational system automatically offers differentiated supports and flexibility. Schools would afford students learning supports based on their strengths and needs. Students have different needs, but no one's need is perceived as "more severe" than others because everyone works toward a unique outcome. Comparison, in this case, would be meaningless. So, there would be no competition, only collaboration. We wouldn't need special education if we didn't confine the educational experience to one approach and method and expect similar outcomes.

While we recognize the harm of "othering," labeling, and stigmatizing students who demonstrate the natural and beautiful diversity of what it means to be human, we also recognize that our efforts to pretend our special education systems won't continue operating as such are harmful. The expectation for all students to demonstrate the same skills simultaneously and in the same way (after being spoon-fed a standardized curriculum) feeds our deficit obsession. Addressing that concern is beyond the scope of this book. We also know a utopian educational system is impossible within our context of standardization and inequity. However, we can still adopt certain aspects of this approach.

We interchange "disability" and "difference" throughout this Reframe and also use the terms "neurodivergent" and "neurotypical." While these terms hold different meanings, in the world of special education, we rely on certain words and diagnoses to "qualify" students for "additional support." We argue that we *can* move away from these labels and the harm they cause while also recognizing the language used in society.

This Reframe, split into eight parts, provides opportunities to disrupt such beliefs by showing the value of each student.

The eight factors shown in Image 6.1 are contributors to our reliance on the deficit within special education, along with eight reframes to begin reducing their harmful impact on our thought processes and actions:

Disabilities	Common strengths	Strength-based learning strategies
ADHD	Creative Imaginative Amazing brainstorming abilities Spontaneous	Deliver content in short, dynamic segments Activate imagination Use humorous teaching approaches Provide hands-on and real-life learning Incorporate movement
Autism	Incredible passions for certain topics Skilled at perceiving details Great engagement with systems, such as machines and computers	Incorporate special interests into learning Allow students to serve as "classroom experts" in their area of interest Use visual models and hands-on learning approaches Emphasize details before presenting the big picture Allow for independent work Allow multiple ways to express knowledge
Dyslexia/ Reading Disabilities	Artistic abilities Strong visual-spatial skills	A multisensory approach to learning Encourage students to visualize what they read Choose reading material that is related to their interests Encourage the use of drawing to demonstrate learning Use graphic organizers

Intellectual Disability			
Down Syndrome	Powerful imitation abilities Amazing humor Charming personalities Strong visual-motor skills	Offer experiential, vivid, hands-on learning approaches Teach through games Use musical, spatial, interpersonal, and kinesthetic learning approaches Include interactive and humorous instructional approaches
Williams Syndrome	Incredible musical/pitch abilities Fantastic oral expression skills	
Fragile X Syndrome	Excellent memories Great imitation skills Strong empathy for others	
Prader-Willi Syndrome	Remarkable ability to solve puzzles	
Emotional and Behavioral Disabilities	Creative Charismatic Playful Often incredibly intelligent	Allow students to express their feelings through creative outlets like painting, drawing, dancing, and music Use role-play to model solutions and teach concepts

Image 6.1: Common strengths and strength-based learning strategies.

While these examples are provided based on the evidence base of common strengths, it is important to remember that each child is unique. We must get to know our students on a personal level.

Deficiency → Abundance

When we hyperfocus on deficits, we forget that all students have strengths.

Renowned dyslexia expert Sally Shaywitz mentions the sea of strengths surrounding the islands of weakness. Suppose we limit our knowledge about students with disabilities to the negatives about their lives—low test scores, low grades, and negative behaviors. In that case, we lose our ability to fully support them. We must understand their strengths, passions, interests, hopes, and goals. Emphasis is placed on *our* awareness as adults. When we highlight each person's strengths, disabling occurs less often. We see the wholeness of our students, not just focusing on one "disabling" feature. We must spend just as much time identifying what they *can* do and how they best demonstrate it.

For example, Byron is a great public speaker, while Kelsie thinks better on paper. When we talk about such differences with each other, we intentionally highlight our strengths over our weaknesses. If someone expected Kelsie to always demonstrate her knowledge verbally without writing, she might present as someone with communication deficits. This would create expectations and assumptions that may not be accurate about Kelsie's true abilities. The same could occur for Byron if he were solely expected to demonstrate knowledge via writing.

Some may consider focusing on strengths as overly optimistic or unrealistic. But is it better to consider students with learning differences or neurodivergence as liabilities or assets? Would you rather have a "rare and beautiful flower" in your classroom or a "broken, damaged problem"? We accept that all flowers and plants have different environmental needs. Our students have unique needs too. This reframe not only changes our perception of students, but it also reminds us that we're responsible for ensuring our rare flowers get the unique support they need. We aren't curing, fixing, repairing, or remediating students.

Expecting Neurotypicality → Expecting Neurodiversity

When we expect students to resemble "normalcy," we don't appreciate differences.

We need to actively remove the idea of a "disability" from our educational dictionaries. Describe students as complex, whole, and vibrant individuals who live and grow on a spectrum of development. They require different environmental contexts to demonstrate their assets. The neurodiversity approach seeks to acknowledge and appreciate the richness and complexity of human nature. Neurodivergence isn't a problem; it's just acceptable human biology. There is no "normal" brain, just as there isn't a "normal" skin tone (despite ever-present socially constructed racism, we *know* that differences in skin tone are biologically natural).

We have been led to believe that people with "disabilities" are incapable of success. When we remind ourselves of neurodiversity, we actively disrupt negative perceptions. We must *expect* and *accept* differences in our classrooms without disabling students. Does a student behave differently than his peers? Great—everyone brings diversity to our classrooms.

Identifying Disabilities → Identifying Needs

When we fixate on diagnoses, we neglect what students need.

When we see an IEP, we immediately generate stereotypical and harmful expectations. What if we viewed special education as solution-seeking instead of problem-solving? What good does a diagnosis do if it does not outline what each student needs? This is especially relevant when preventing a misdiagnosis in the guise of ensuring students receive additional support. With Kelsie's writing strengths and speaking weaknesses, it would be unnecessary to deem Kelsie's speaking weakness as a disability or deficit. We know she would benefit from support or modifications to communicate her thoughts acceptably. Under our current systems, Kelsie may be put into a separate program that continuously forced her to speak publicly to strengthen that deficiency. She would feel "less than" because written language was unvalued.

This reframe also allows us to identify students based on what they *need* and not what they *are*.

Language and perception are so important when reviewing IEPs. When we label a student with a learning disability, we center on the student as the problem. Suppose we instead describe a student who benefits from small-group instruction and learns best with multisensory approaches, and we notice a strength in oral communication. In that case, we have identified solutions the school can offer.

Schools hire support staff members to support the needs of students in special education. This drives the deficit approach by requiring an assessment for disabilities and providing services solely based on deficiencies. These individuals are not to blame. They're using specific instruments, tools, and operations identified by their organizations to do their jobs. Special education teachers, psychologists, counselors, social workers, speech and language therapists, occupational therapists, and paraprofessionals need to reframe their work to support our students—as humans with strengths and needs just like everyone else.

Individual Focus → Environmental Focus

When we assume disabilities exist within an individual, we forget about the role we and the environment play.

To successfully support the diverse learning needs of our students, *we* must change the learning environment. *We* must build environments that fit unique strengths rather than expecting students to bend and mold their bodies and minds to fit into our unsuitable environments.

Kelsie and Byron's strengths highlight how *environments* and *expectations* often lead to disabling. If verbal communication was standard and written communication wasn't offered as an option, we have created a disability where it didn't exist. We do the same thing if we don't offer ramps, Braille, subtitles, communication devices, and interpreters. Just because a person is blind, deaf, or nonverbal does not mean they can't comprehend and communicate with others. Imagine that the daily supports we use to navigate the world are not present. If the power goes out at nighttime, someone who is not blind will struggle with navigating the space. Someone who is blind would have an advantage. When our environments don't match our needs, we appear disabled.

This also happens with students who are nonverbal—we make assumptions about their intelligence, abilities, and capabilities for success when we do not offer suitable alternatives to verbal communication. We must assess our environments and expectations for potentially disabling features. A specific environment can be helpful for some and hurtful for others, but we *can* modify the environment to support different strengths.

Maybe you concentrate best while sitting still and maintaining eye contact with the presenter or material, but another person concentrates best while tapping a pencil, pacing, or doodling while listening. When we constrain an individual's ability to learn in the way they learn best, we feed our reliance on deficit thinking. Use the following reframes to redirect your energy:

- Rather than saying, "They can't sit still for longer than fifteen minutes," say, "They learn best when offered an opportunity to move around or sit in flexible seating."

- Rather than saying, "They can't remain on task in class," say, "They focus best when offered frequent breaks, using fidgets, and if you don't expect them to look directly at the presenter."

Our classroom structures, instructional techniques, behavior management systems, and classroom cultures and climates often lead to disabling. While it is uncomfortable to consider ourselves as the ones doing the "disabling," it is a way to regain classroom power and control. If we can cause it, we can also remove it. Many approaches learned in teacher preparation programs rely on a uniform approach to navigating extremely diverse student needs. We need to unlearn what we've learned.

Rather than relying on a list of evidence-based interventions or approaches that don't individualize the learning process, we must use each student's unique strengths to support them in nontraditional ways. Universal Design for Learning (UDL) aims to remove the barriers of traditional schools. UDL focuses on the "what" of learning, the "how" of learning, and the "why" of learning. It changes how students present information and express their knowledge, accommodating learning differences.

The more we reiterate to students that there is no one way to learn, the more we normalize differences. How can you undo your understanding of what the learning environment must look like to reduce your impact in contributing to disabling spaces?

Leveled Learning → Personal Growth

When we compare students to each other, we minimize individual success

In Reframe 3, we explain the harm of our data metrics. It would be silly to compare Kelsie's growth in public speaking to Byron's. Byron will likely grow at a quicker pace. If we perceive his pace as the norm, he may be considered average. We would consider Kelsie deficient or well below average, even if she makes substantial growth.

We do not need to lower expectations, though. This approach can lead to high and achievable expectations for students. When we cater student goals and objectives to their unique strengths, we deemphasize a lack of growth toward an artificial expectation. In this regard, IEP goals would ensure that all students have opportunities to bloom at their own pace, not being higher or lower than a set standard.

Assuming Failure → Assuming Success

When we adopt a maximum threshold for students, we don't give them a chance at success.

We do not expect many students with disabilities to be successful after secondary school, so we do not discuss future aspirations with them. When we reframe and focus on student strengths and interests, we can encourage them to aspire to careers that suit those strengths and interests.

We can identify neurodivergent adults in the community or popular culture as positive role models. This aids in undoing the deficit narrative, allowing students to reclaim their power and expectations for success.

Sameness → Creativity

When we require uniformity, we miss out on communal learning opportunities.

People often perceive special education as a "place." Students cannot operate in our disabling environments, so they are to go to a special place where someone can address their needs until they learn how to fit into our environment. This belief is incredibly harmful. All students, neurodivergent or neurotypical, *can* thrive collaboratively. They learn when exposed to people who learn, think, and look different than them. We possess an infinite number of strengths at the group level. Kelsie and Byron offer a rich set of strengths when working *together*. We worked to set goals based on our individual and pair-level strengths. No one felt inferior for having a different set of strengths or needs. This is the beauty of human diversity and human difference.

When this mentality is adopted in the classroom, we allow all our students, neurotypical or neurodivergent, able-bodied or disabled, the ability to contribute something meaningful to our environment. We must allow our students to collaboratively identify their strengths and weaknesses and share opportunities. What if, instead of separating students by differences, we grouped our students because of their differences and allowed them to learn, teach, and support one another to enhance the learning environment for everyone?

Adults as Experts → Students as Experts

We miss an important perspective when we assume we know what's best.

How often do we truly involve students in discussions of their strengths and needs? They may attend IEP meetings as witnesses, but the entire special education process often does not involve students. We resort to the deficit model when we don't allow our students to share their needs and perspectives. If we adopted a strength-based approach to assessing our students, it wouldn't feel so awkward to share results with them. Students are the experts of themselves. To know what is happening, why it's happening, and how to identify and implement a solution, we must involve them.

WHAT YOU CAN DO TOMORROW

Now that we've reviewed our eight factors and reframes, what does this look like in practice? And how can we make small strides toward change? We present the following actions you can take right away.

- **Review the IEPs of your students in special education and intentionally look for strengths.** Suppose it's hard for you to find any mention of strengths in student IEPs. It may be important to consider reaching out to the IEP team and a school psychologist to discuss changes that can be made to more intentionally focus on strengths, whether through formal or informal assessment.

- **Implement an activity where all your students figure out what kind of learners they are.** You can find many free online tools and questionnaires that identify the best ways people learn. Check out educationplanner.org for one example. Facilitate a conversation about how all students learn differently or the same. Talk about what they've learned about each other! This is an easy way to introduce the idea of neurodiversity and normalize differences.

- **Follow up with previous students who received special education services in your building to see what they've been up to post-school.** This holds us accountable for determining whether our students are being successful and allows us to reframe our expectations when we learn about successes. Consider inviting previous students to speak with current students.

- **Start and end with the positives at your next IEP meeting.** Too often, our IEP meetings are filled with negative references about student performance on tests and assignments. We must intentionally shine a light on what our students can do well. Just one positive interaction can drastically change the essence of a meeting.

A BLUEPRINT FOR FULL IMPLEMENTATION

Step 1: Anticipate neurodiversity and variance in student needs.

At the beginning of the year, we expect physical, mental, and behavioral differences among our students. Typically, teachers review their classroom list for students who have IEPs. This review can create anxiety. The more students with IEPs, the more concern a teacher may feel about their ability to be successful that year. But what if we remember that all students, regardless of identified disabilities, have different needs? In contrast, we can't expect all students in "general education" to have wildly different needs than students who have been identified with a disability.

This mindset shift reminds us that we will be welcoming a group of vibrant and unique students into our classrooms with differences and similarities alike. We are less likely to problematize these differences because we were already prepared for a variation of needs. This expectation also allows us to remember that we need to offer a variety of strategies and approaches to support the unique needs of our students. This is not to discount the needs of our neurodiverse students but to reframe the way we perceive those needs at the beginning of the year to prepare ourselves for an expectation of differentiation.

Step 2: Develop your philosophies of abundance and success.

There are many ways to shift from a philosophy of deficiency to a philosophy of abundance. The most important way involves humanizing our students who have learning differences. Rather than assuming we know everything there is to know about them after learning about their identified disability, we must establish genuine relationships with them to understand their interests and strengths. We must give them the opportunity and space to understand themselves. Perhaps your student with autism has an amazing interest in computer programming.

- How can you build on this strength to support their learning in other ways?

- In what ways can you allow this student to teach the other students in your class about computer programming?

- What other skills or assets stem from this skill that they can build upon?

Image 6.1 presents typical strengths for the most common disabilities we see within our schools, along with strength-based learning approaches. Our sharing of these strength-based learning strategies is so you can conceptualize what learning can and should look like for all students, rather than following a prescription for use with students of certain disabilities. We sought examples to change your perception of why a student may not be as successful in your room as others. It allows you to remember the role you play in shaping the environment for all your students and providing opportunities for students to learn how they learn best—and advocate for themselves.

You can further develop your philosophy of abundance and success by inviting successful neurodivergent adults from your local community to visit your schools, share their stories, and connect with neurodivergent students. Students may identify with positive role models when we mention notable, effective people who also happened to be identified as having a disability. You could incorporate this as an activity where you assign students to research notable people with disabilities. The more we showcase the strengths of neurodivergent individuals and individuals with learning differences and broadcast their capabilities for success despite (or sometimes because of) these differences, the more we actively chip away at deficit beliefs about neurodivergent people. See Image 6.2.

Learning Disability	Autism	ADHD	Intellectual Disability	Emotional Disability
Whoopi Goldberg (Actor)	Albert Einstein (Scientist & Mathematician)	Michael Phelps (Olympic Swimmer)	Gloria Lenhoff (Singer-Sings in 25 different languages)	Angelina Jolie (Actress)
Pablo Picasso (Painter)	Bill Gates (Co-founder of Microsoft)	Leonardo da Vinci (Artist)	Sujeet Desai (Musician)	Vincent Van Gogh (Artist)
Muhammad Ali (Professional Boxer)	Temple Grandin (Scientist/Writer)	Justin Timberlake (Singer/Actor)	Jason Kingsley (Writer/Sesame Street Star)	Abraham Lincoln (16th President of the US)
Tim Tebow (NFL Player)	Michelangelo (Sculptor, Painter, Architect, Poet)	Mozart (Composer)	Chris Burke (Actor, Author, Musician)	J. K. Rowling (Writer)
George Washington (1st US President)	Isaac Newton (Mathematician, Astronomer, Physicist)	Walt Disney (Founder of Disneyland)	Jane Cameron (Tapestry Artist)	Barbra Streisand (Singer/Actor)

Steve Jobs (Founder of Apple)	Jerry Seinfeld (Comedian)	Michael Jordan (NBA Player)	Bernadette Resha (Painter/Artist)	Jackson Pollock (Painter)
Magic Johnson (NBA Player)	Satoshi Tajiri (Creator of Pokemon)	Jim Carrey (Actor/ Comedian/ Producer)	Jackie Barrett (Special Olympian Power Weightlifter)	Mike Tyson (Professional Boxer)
Octavia Spencer (Actress)	Elon Musk (Billionaire Entrepreneur)	Will Smith (Actor/ Producer/ Rapper)	Scott Rohrer (Special Olympian Golfer)	Calvin Coolidge (30th President of the US)
Anderson Cooper (Broadcaster)	Steven Spielberg (Film Director)	John F. Kennedy (35th President of the US)	Gretchen Josephson (Writer/Poet)	Julian Huxley (Biologist)
Tommy Hilfiger (Fashion Designer	Thomas Edison (Inventor)	Simone Biles (Olympian Gymnast)	Susan Harrington (MTV Star)	John Rockefeller (Businessman/ Founder of Oil Industry)

Image 6.2: Successful and notable people with learning differences or neurodivergence.*

*It is important to remember that each child is unique, and one cannot simply rely on a list of people with one similar characteristic. We must get to know our students on a personal level to understand their passions and dreams. Rather, this table is designed to chip away at the adult and student belief that students with disabilities are unlikely to be successful.

You can cultivate aspirations for students with learning differences. See the table in Image 6.3 for potential careers that neurodivergent youth may aspire to, based on common strengths. Remember: these are examples, *not the only options.* The last thing we want to do is contribute to the idea of a "single story." Rather, we present these to aid in reframing the deficit-based assumptions you've likely adopted over time. They serve as a stepping stone for brainstorming student strengths, along with ways they can use those skill sets to aspire toward future careers or jobs.

Disabilities	Potential future careers based on common strengths
ADHD	Entrepreneur, journalist, building contractor, athlete/coach
Autism	Web page designer, video game designer, auto mechanic, animal trainer, library assistant, bank teller, statistician, assembly line worker
Intellectual Disabilities	Animal caretaker, library assistant, store clerk, cook, cashier, hospital attendant, furniture refinisher
Dyslexia/ Reading Disabilities	Animator, engineer, artist, interior decorator, graphic software designer, pilot, surgeon, photographer, inventor, architect

Image 6.3: Potential future careers of students with identified "disabilities" based on common research-based strengths.

*While these examples are provided based on the evidence base of common strengths, it is important to remember that each child is unique. We must get to know our students on a personal level.

Step 3: Get creative with your environment.

Here is a brief example of a special education approach in France called APATE *(Association Pour l'Accueil de Tous le Enfants)* [Association for the Reception of All Children]. It operates from a collectivist integration approach to special education that views differences as an effect of groups coming together.

This classroom is not a general education classroom nor a special education classroom; it is a classroom for teaching all children. This approach allows us to realize that "normal classrooms" are classrooms that meet the needs of all students. Rather than students with disabilities as "guests" in "normal" classrooms (where they should be grateful for a chance to engage with "normal" students), we need to shift toward an approach where all labels come together as equals that inform everyone's learning.

When creating an anti-deficit environment for students with learning differences, the goal is not to assimilate students into the environment. The goal is to change the environment, not the students. And the best way to do this is through our knowledge of their unique strengths. With those in mind, we design environments that afford the best learning experience.

Step 4: Collaborate with students on goals and progress.

Thomas Armstrong, a neurodiversity guru, presents a protocol for strength-based IEP meetings that intentionally involves students, families, and teams in considering the success and goals of students. Consider asking students the following questions (adapted from Armstrong's protocol). Remember to incorporate their feedback into their IEP.

- Tell me about some of your successes this year.
- What have you done well?
- What worked for you this year?
- What do you think led you to your successes?
- What do you think you'd love most to do when you grow up?
- What is your goal in life?
- What do you think you need to be doing right now to do what you love most?
- What have you done so far to reach this goal?
- What do you need from others to get to this goal?

When we ask these questions, we can facilitate a conversation that involves our students in decisions. We also reiterate our high expectations of their ability to achieve goals. When we gain student buy-in about what they strive toward, we can reach them collaboratively.

OVERCOMING PUSHBACK

As educators, we receive many messages about disabilities and mental illness that can be difficult to shift away from in our roles. It can be incredibly challenging to adopt a strength-based approach in a world where we have been conditioned to think of disabilities as weaknesses. In this section, you will find a few potential thoughts you may face as you grapple with this approach to your work.

Shouldn't I be realistic about the future potential of my students with disabilities? There is a serious difference between being realistic and operating from a deficit-based perspective. You cannot incorporate a strength-based approach and philosophy of abundance without realism or else you risk setting up our students for another type of failure. Our approach should not minimize student weaknesses, but we should also not maximize those weaknesses. There are ways to recognize student needs in tandem with strengths. Cultivating inspiration is never unrealistic. All it takes is one person to believe in someone to change their life trajectory. That's as real as it gets.

I'm not a special educator. Why is this my job? To this, we remind you that as educators, we support the needs of *all* students. We cannot pick and choose which students we work with. This reframe also reminds us that simply referring a student to the special education team doesn't absolve us of the responsibility to develop meaningful relationships, regardless of need or perceived difference. Some students may challenge you in ways you never thought imaginable. However, we must always remember that the more blame we place on the child, the more frustrated we will become. When we remember that we can make a difference, we slowly but surely broaden our locus of control.

I don't mean to be deficit-based, but I truly struggle to identify the strengths of some students. Sometimes we need to redefine what we are looking for when we say we are looking for "strengths." Every student has strengths. We have just been trained to only look for and value ableist, racist, and classist strengths. The more we normalize an emphasis on nontraditional strengths and incorporate such strengths into our learning spaces, the more strengths we will see within our students. Armstrong created the Neurodiversity Strengths Checklist (presented in his book *Neurodiversity in the Classroom*), where he shares 165 strengths in the following seventeen categories:

- Personal strengths

- Communication strengths

- Social strengths

- Emotional strengths

- Cognitive strengths

- Creative strengths

- Literacy strengths

- Logical strengths

- Visual-spatial strengths

- Physical strengths

- Dexterity strengths

- Musical strengths

- Nature strengths

- High-tech strengths

- Spiritual strengths

- Cultural strengths

- Other strengths

We argue that every child has a plethora of varied strengths. We challenge you to expand your thinking about strengths.

THE REFRAME IN ACTION

The three most commonly identified disabilities in school settings are autism, specific learning disability (SLD) in reading, and attention deficit hyperactivity disorder (ADHD), which is commonly categorized as an "other health impairment" (OHI). We suggest positive ways to alter the environment for students with these classifications.

Scenario 1: Willow

Willow, a seventh grader, has struggled with reading since kindergarten. Although they're in seventh grade, their performance on standardized assessments reveals a second grade level. Willow also struggles with spelling, written expression, and writing conventions. They possess exceptional drawing abilities and often sketch during class, producing lifelike images of various animals.

In a traditional special education space, Willow's IEP team would identify deficiencies and a special education classification, likely providing pull-out special education supports to "catch Willow up" to same-age peers as quickly as possible. During pull-out sessions, Willow would likely receive a standardized and specialized curriculum in a special education classroom that focuses on low level and abstract reading strategies, such as phoneme isolation and decoding. The general education classroom would provide some accommodations, but ultimately, Willow would receive the same instruction as their peers. Due to the IEP, the teacher would likely lower expectations for Willow's success.

However, when adopting an abundant view of Willow, we focus on the skills they possess, including excellent math computation and geometry skills. A review of Willow's special education testing identifies visual-spatial strengths. The team also discovers that Willow has an incredible ability to remember the visual details of animals. They realize that Willow is motivated by learning and reading about animals to inform their drawing.

In this narrative, Willow's team keeps them in the general education classroom full time and adopts strength-based learning strategies that build upon their visual-spatial and artistic abilities. Willow serves as the teaching assistant during art class and enjoys supporting their peers with project initiation. Teachers allow Willow to use a speech-to-text reader for all math word problems and assignments that require applied reading.

Willow combines the act of strengthening their reading skills with learning about and drawing animals. They enroll in a community college-level drawing course to strengthen their artistic skills. Willow works on writing stories to describe their drawings. Rather than comparing Willow's progress to same-age peers, they graph progress toward their spelling, sentence-writing, and reading fluency with a self-created tool. Willow plays a role in all aspects of the development of their plan—motivated to make progress because of it.

Scenario 2: Ava

Ava, a second grader, recently received a diagnosis of ADHD-combined type presentation. Her mother is not interested in medication because of Ava's age. Ava's ADHD diagnosis manifests as fidgeting in her seat, frequently getting up, and blurting out answers in class. While she has great ideas, she struggles to organize them on paper and benefits from repeated directions. Because she struggles with initiating and completing tasks, she is often required to finish her work during recess as a consequence. A traditional special education approach would likely involve the creation of a behavior intervention plan that seeks to increase her ability to stay on task in class, reduce her out-of-seat and shout-out behavior, and improve her ability to initiate tasks independently. When she meets her daily goals, she could be afforded an opportunity for a break.

However, when we adopt an abundant view of Ava, we realize that her brain works best when she can move her body. We recognize that when she "blurts out" an answer, she demonstrates her excitement for learning. We realize that while Ava takes a longer time to produce a physical outcome than some of her peers, she always demonstrates her knowledge eventually. This reframe allows us to see the environmental changes we can easily make to set Ava up for success.

Rather than implementing a behavior intervention plan to minimize the characteristics that make Ava herself, her teacher decides to implement a culture of flexible seating throughout the entire class. Students can sit on the floor, in bean bag chairs, on a bouncy ball, in a traditional chair, or at a standing workstation. Ava's teacher is surprised to see that most of her students benefit from this, as she presumed it would cause disruption. Ava's teacher also began allowing students to bring in or use approved fidgets such as squeeze balls, fidget spinners, and poppers, which also benefits most of her students. While she was worried that the students would take advantage of the toys, she soon realized that only the students who needed the fidgets used them after the "honeymoon" phase wore off.

Students now volunteer to be "roamers" during independent and group work, where they walk around and brainstorm with peers who need help. This is especially helpful for Ava when she volunteers, as she gets to glimpse the ideas of others. They aid her in formulating her own approaches. Ava's teacher also now encourages her students to "turn and talk" every five to ten minutes to ponder any discussion topic.

Finally, Ava no longer loses recess as a punishment because her team recognizes the importance of movement. Rather, Ava's teacher checks in with her periodically to verbally brainstorm with her and aid her in going in a direction that allows her to express herself, whether verbally, via an audio recording, or on paper.

Scenario 3: Muhammad

Muhammad, a kindergarten student, begins his first year of traditional schooling. His diagnosis of autism manifests as a preferred interest in independent play, greater success in predictable and low-sensory-induced environments, and a fascination with vehicles. While Muhammad doesn't engage in social speaking as much as his same-age peers, he enjoys singing his favorite songs (often during "inappropriate" times) and echoing what his peers say. Muhammad has an amazing memory and has already developed many rote academic skills—he knows his ABCs and can count to one hundred.

A traditional special education approach would likely involve intensified and individualized support to "improve" Muhammad's behaviors to be similar to his same-age peers. That may involve speech therapy, where Muhammad learns appropriate verbal communication and how to express his needs in neurotypical ways. It may involve encouraging Muhammad and his peers to play together and offering praise when Muhammad interacts with his peers. It may involve allowing Muhammad free time to play with his cars when he successfully reduces his echolalic behaviors or reduces his singing behaviors during inappropriate times.

However, when we adopt an abundant view of Muhammad, we consider supports for him, but we also consider the environmental factors needed to make learning a more comfortable space for him. We consider approaches that increase Muhammad's classmates' understanding of neurodiversity and autism. For example, rather than seeking to assimilate Muhammad into the classroom, we begin the year with the expectation that the environment will assimilate to Muhammad and to the neurodiversity of the other students.

We do not force Muhammad to verbally communicate unless he chooses to. We do not force Muhammad to play with his peers if he would rather play alone. We teach all students in the classroom a few basic words in sign language that Muhammad seems to rely on. Muhammad's speech supports focus on ensuring that he can communicate his needs in whatever way is most beneficial for him.

Muhammad uses an electronic communication system to express when he needs to go to the bathroom. He often leads the class in singing his favorite song, "Old MacDonald Had a Farm," and in singing the ABCs. His classmates know that although he doesn't look at them, it doesn't mean he isn't enjoying himself. The students in Muhammad's class regularly talk about how we communicate with each other, play, and learn in the classroom. Muhammad is not singled out as "different" because other students prefer to play alone and benefit from a picture schedule.

The teacher implements Muhammad's interest in cars, car parts, and trains into his learning tasks and the learning tasks at the group level. When Muhammad engages in stimming behaviors, his peers focus on the different ways we regulate ourselves to feel better when we are overwhelmed, feel too energetic, or experience anxiety. We may take deep breaths, shake our hands, hum or sing to ourselves, or squeeze a stress ball. The students in Muhammad's class realize that this is how he takes care of his needs. Students welcome Muhammad, and he holds a space in the classroom community. By the end of the year, Muhammad mutually develops a friendship with another student.

We must not fall into the trap of deficiency when working with our students receiving special education services. While our systems are rooted in deficit thinking, we can still strive to change the way we describe their needs and alter our environments to support them. We can see the whole child and ensure that all students can develop and build upon their strengths, realizing the benefit neurodiversity brings into our classrooms. We can allow those assets to drive our environments of collaboration and creativity.

REFRAME
7

TAP INTO SCHOOLWIDE STRENGTHS
Strength in Community

A lot of our students and families have amazing assets that are beyond what we often value in the White-centered education realm, and those often aren't acknowledged, valued, or tapped into.

— KRISTA RICE, SCHOOL PSYCHOLOGIST

THE BELIEF:
WE OPERATE WITHIN AT-RISK SCHOOLS

"WE NEED TO close the achievement gap."

"We need to improve our test scores."

"Our students have to know all of this before the test."

If you've made it this far in the book, you hopefully realize that these are deficit-based phrases. Deficit thinking tells us that students are mere numbers that define our success as a school rather than whole children with individual sets of strengths, assets, and abilities that contribute to our collective strengths.

We are led to believe that success is determined by a student's ability to master a predefined and White-centered set of ideals at an arbitrary rate that must be regurgitated back to us at one specific point in time and in one specific format.

"This student isn't a good fit for our school." "Some students are incapable of being successful in our school." How often have you heard educators say comments like these about a student or group of students?

We hear this when speaking about a child who requires more behavioral support than "other" students need. We hear this when speaking of most of our students identified as having disabilities. We hear this when speaking about students who have transferred from a "bad" location. We even hear this when speaking about students learning English as a second language. What has led to the idea that some students are unworthy of occupying our spaces? And why haven't our schools adapted enough to be a good fit for the diverse needs of our students? A simple flip in language can open the door for deeper reflection.

As Dr. Cyndy Alvarez, a school psychologist, says, "Deficit thinking is a byproduct of White supremacy in schooling."

White supremacy is so embedded in our schools that it prevents us from fully seeing our students' strengths. The foundation of White supremacy notions in our schools continues to only value specific characteristics, leading us to believe that anyone who challenges these notions is the problem. Today, we continue to see the residue of the belief that anyone who isn't a White, middle-class, able-bodied, cisgender, male is deficient—and unworthy of education.

Drs. Kenneth Jones and Tema Okun identify fifteen characteristics in organizations that operate from a White supremacy culture. We argue that the following characteristics show up in our schools, leading to spaces where deficit thinking can flourish: perfectionism, defensiveness, worship of the written word, paternalism/power hoarding, and individualism.

We need to create new structures that are welcoming to students, encourage their input, and acknowledge their competence. This requires a shift from a pedagogy of compliance to a pedagogy of voice and trust. It requires the following cultural shifts:

- Perfectionism → Learning from Mistakes

- Defensiveness → Receptiveness

- Worship of the Written Word → Worship of the Student Word

- Paternalism → Shared Power

- Individualism → Collectivism

WSC Characteristic	How It Shows Up
Perfectionism	Refusal to accept anything short of perfection. Making a mistake is synonymous with being a mistake. Heightened appreciation for people who fit the "perfect" student or staff mold. Little value for progress.
Defensiveness	Criticism of those with power is viewed as rude and threatening. People respond to new initiatives or ideas with defensiveness. Maintaining the status quo. Discomfort results in blaming the person for raising the issue.
Worship of the Written Word	If it's not written down, it doesn't exist. Ignoring other ways information can be shared. "There is only one right way to do things."
Paternalism/Power Hoarding	Those with power don't find it important or necessary to understand other viewpoints. Those without power don't know how decisions are made. Those with power perceive suggestions as a reflection of their leadership (or see others as inexperienced and ill-informed).
Individualism	Little value in working as part of a team. Competition is valued over cooperation.

Examples	Harm Caused
Students who meet benchmarks at the "normed" rate are preferred over students who make progress at a slower rate.	Anyone who demonstrates "imperfection" is viewed as inferior; this reinforces deficit thinking, especially with historically marginalized groups
If a student shares that they experienced a microaggression by a teacher, the teacher blames the student for reacting the way they did.	Problems go unaddressed, leading to a culture where people are afraid to express their opinions.
Blanket curriculums are implemented in schools because these are the "only" ways to teach our students, without room for creativity.	Students who do not learn in a direct, uniform, or linear manner are viewed as inferior.
Students do not take part in decisions that impact their everyday experiences. Admin and teachers assume that they know what is best.	Creates a culture of toxicity and fear. Students have no control over their learning and are less likely to enjoy school.
Students must demonstrate their knowledge independently. Shared ideas are perceived as "cheating."	People from backgrounds that value community are perceived as inferior, leading to isolation.

Image 7.1: White supremacist culture and deficit thinking in schools.

Now, you may be wondering how we rid ourselves of these ideologies that are blinding us from seeing the whole student. We argue throughout this book that all our students, especially those from historically marginalized and minoritized backgrounds, bring several strengths that can transform our schools from being "at-risk buildings" to spaces where students and adults can flourish.

THE REFRAME:
TAP INTO SCHOOLWIDE STRENGTHS

"Imagine the pressure to be perfect and good at everything, and if you're not, you're low—and that is a deficit label."
— WENDY TURNER, TEACHER

How do we create a culture that allows the strengths of our historically marginalized and minoritized youth to be valued and sustained?

How do we intentionally implement systems that show all our students that they matter? Because many of the practices we still use today are rooted in White supremacist culture and have the expectation of only catering to one type of child, we need changes that reflect our societal goal of supporting all children within the community.

Gallup identified the following four factors as important in leading to student success and well-being:

- **Engagement**: student involvement in and enthusiasm for school

- **Hope**: the ideas and energy students have for the future

- **Belonging**: feeling accepted and included as part of the school

- **Social-emotional learning**: learning to understand and manage emotions, including positive relationships

In examining these four areas, let's acknowledge what is not on this list—grades, test scores, the ability to demonstrate "positive behaviors," and the ability to "comply" with adult demands. The traditional methods educators have relied on to determine whether a student will be successful or not are *not* working. And they're not working because of the lack of student voice and collaboration. When we focus on how our students feel and what they need, we can combine both to set them up for success. This, in combination with collaborative and flexible learning procedures, is key. To tap into the strengths of all our students, we need to include them in our decision-making—feel free to refer back to Reframe 3, where we discuss HUMANE data collection. Consider this Reframe an extension.

Rigid age-graded curriculum, normative testing protocols, and "ability" grouping will never allow for true integration and appreciation of the student diversity within our buildings. We need to create new structures that are welcoming to students, encourage their input, and acknowledge their competence, especially for the students we've failed for a long time. To implement this reframe in our schools requires a shift from a pedagogy of compliance to a pedagogy of voice and trust. It requires the following cultural shifts:

- Perfectionism → Learning from Mistakes
- Defensiveness → Receptiveness
- Worship of the Written Word → Worship of the Student Word
- Paternalism → Shared Power
- Individualism → Collectivism

Learning from Mistakes

One of the biggest contributors to White supremacy is the expectation of "perfection." In schools, we expect perfection from our students in their abilities to demonstrate specific behaviors and knowledge at precise times. We reprimand them through grades or referrals when they don't demonstrate such performance. We expect educators to be perfect as well.

Expecting perfection leads to a lack of vulnerability, a lack of anticipation for bumps in the road, and breeding grounds for deficit thinking. We must expect mistakes and use them as learning experiences. When we do so, we develop a culture of appreciation. We teach our students that it's okay to not know something and that it's okay to ask for help. We recognize that sometimes mistakes lead to positive results.

When we normalize mistakes, we prevent our students from internalizing deficit assumptions about themselves. Normalizing mistakes and honoring a culture of growth mindset leads to respectful spaces. When we are patient with ourselves and our students, we allow students to show up as their authentic selves. This approach strengthens relationships and reiterates that critical feedback is never ill-intended and is necessary for growth. This leads to fewer opportunities to blame ourselves or our students. We can foster equitable spaces of learning where strengths authentically develop.

When we embrace mistakes, we separate people from their mistakes.

Receptiveness

Defensiveness is often the root of a culture of deficit thinking. We become self-protective when challenged to consider our contributions to an outcome or confronted with challenges to our power. We must understand the link between defensiveness and fear, and talk about what we fear losing when we become vulnerable. We actively do away with our deficit and White-centered schools when we acknowledge the existing issues without becoming defensive. Change at the school level cannot happen unless we *talk* about it at the school level.

We can embrace critical discussions about deficit thinking, White supremacy, and how these ideologies show up in our schools and our work with students and families—often unconsciously. We can acknowledge and accept our place in a system of blame. Another important part of acceptance is preparing for and embracing conflict as it arises. We can listen to concerns raised by our students or staff that uncover serious systemic issues. We recommend the *Courageous Conversations About Race* book and resources as a starting point for this process.

As Wendy Turner says, "Norms developed at the classroom, team, and school level have to disallow deficit language and get at the heart of deficit thinking, implementing tools and experiences that change mindset[s] because that is where it all starts."

One cannot do this under a culture of defensiveness.

Worship of the Student Word

Our current school systems allow testing schedules and mandates to drive our curriculum, instructional approaches, and policy-driven interactions with students. We operate in a space not centered on the needs of our stakeholders. It centers on testing corporations—that often don't have any vested interest in our well-being. When we continue to worship this approach, we feed deficit thinking. However, when we let our students drive our approaches, we cultivate their strengths and assets along with their learning needs. We improve their learning experiences and our teaching experiences by taking away the guesswork. These two ideologies can coexist if we are willing to be vulnerable with our students about what we do and don't have control over. This also teaches them societal decision-making and how to advocate for their needs.

There are so many ways to get to the goal of successfully educating our students and helping them demonstrate learning and growth without just worshipping the written word. When we include our students and families in problem-solving and implement their suggestions, we demonstrate that we care about what they have to say and allow them to be accountable for their learning.

Ashley Tucker describes the importance of giving students flexibility to demonstrate their learning, allowing students to lead the way. "So, allowing students to make a video, make a rap, write a poem, draw a picture, realizing that there's a lot of different ways to get students to meet the learning objective or the learning goal for that day."

Uncovering stories of hope and harm directly from the source humanizes our students. The more we allow our students to aid us in analyzing their schooling experiences, the more heightened we become to strategies that humanize the learning process. We teach them that school officials don't know everything, and *that's okay!* We improve their learning experiences and our teaching experiences by eliminating guesses.

Shared Power

We have many teams in our schools—leadership, positive behavior, and student intervention teams. But we leave out the people directly impacted by our decisions—the students.

Why don't we involve students in conversations about their education? Why do we assume that we are the experts in cultivating success for students?

When we teach in ways that allow us to be the only "master," we believe that we are *the* "master." We can tap into student strengths when we allow for opportunities that show us how much they know. It challenges the deficit belief that we know more than our students.

As Safir and Dugan note, we must shift from a pedagogy of compliance to a pedagogy of voice. Most schools operate from a pedagogy of compliance that involves teacher-led instruction, students looking to the teacher as the expert, and teachers carrying the cognitive load. Compliance-driven pedagogy leads to student disengagement. It also impacts our perception of "at-risk" students.

On the other hand, a pedagogy of voice shifts the student's locus of learning and power. It decenters compliance, grading, "answers," competition, and all features that uphold the harmful and outdated testing-industrial complex. Most importantly, it values and centers on the needs of those who are often not afforded a seat at the table. This shift is especially important for Black, Brown, and Indigenous students who have historically been led to believe that they don't belong in learning spaces fueled by White supremacy and deficit thinking.

As Cain states, "Consistently, teachers come in and say, 'This is my room, do what I say ...' It [reminds] me of plantation-type work; it reminds me of master serve—that only you can be the purveyor of information in here. So, one thing I had teachers do is create something called the genius hour where [the teachers] sit down and [the students] get up and present things ... this is about teaching them how to do this. ... Maybe they haven't had a chance to learn how to debate and haven't had a chance to have a Socratic seminar ... Teach them those methods and then let them use them to talk about things they want to talk about."

Tucker expands on this line of thinking: "I have to know you. I have to understand you so that we're able to do this work. So, I really think it's taking a step back, scaling things back, and thinking about who this student is, what are some of the experiences that they've had before they even came to me, and how can I create this learning environment or co-create this learning environment in order to lead to their success?"

This is also the case at the staff level. As William Blake says, "When you first get to leadership, you often have the mindset that 'You do what I say,' but as I grew older, I had to learn that you have to truly give directives and instructions based off what people do well because when you do that, they work ten times harder because they have something intrinsically motivated for them to succeed in what they do, which ultimately turns into having an impact for kids."

Collectivism

Deficit thinking will forever thrive in a space that values individualism and competitiveness. The White-centered notion of being "the best" or "better" emphasizes a lack of respect for people who value collectivism. Collectivism places the value of the group over the value of the individual. This separation has fed the deficit narrative that children with "different" cultural backgrounds don't belong in our classrooms. When we intentionally foster community and acceptance of differences within our schools and classrooms, we actively deny deficit thinking a seat at the table. We can place just as much emphasis on how our students and staff work together as we do on their abilities to work independently. Educators should avoid working in silos, and so should our students!

Collective learning is incredibly powerful. Think about brainstorming sessions

> We must cultivate communities of admiration and collaboration where we don't just "accept" and "include" people *despite* their differences but rather admire them *because of* their differences.

where multiple people contribute their perspectives and ideas. Children are thirsty for knowledge and fresh ideas. We do a disservice to all students—yes, especially those from privileged backgrounds—when we don't allow the diversity of our students to shine through in our practices.

We must cultivate communities of admiration and collaboration where we don't just "accept" and "include" people *despite* their differences but rather admire them *because of* their differences. Spaces that don't admire difference lose out on the authentically diverse perspectives and experiences that all students contribute to the learning environment. When we collectively come together and authentically share these perspectives, everyone benefits.

Another benefit of a collectivist approach is shared responsibility. When we teach students that they are not competitors, we create a culture of accountability. If there is an area where a student is struggling, how can we collectively build them up?

William Black says, "I definitely believe in using ... that Gallup StrengthsFinder's tool to truly identify and maximize the strength of the community. And when I say community, it's the folks that we work with. It's our students; it's our parents."

See Reframe 5 for approaches to assess student strengths and creative uses for identifying strengths. You can develop a community where all students contribute something to the classroom based on their strengths.

A culture of accountability and collectivism must also occur at the staff level. Pamela Tucker says, "Schools must provide professional development that makes teachers aware of deficit thinking. Schools must also provide PD around strategies that will make changes to their teacher planning practices as well as instructional practices and hold teachers accountable for the implementation of the strategies." When we implement this approach at the system level, we create spaces of collaboration and accountability.

So, what happens when we shift toward anti-deficit practices and anti-White supremacist culture? William Blake shares what happens when we do all these things.

"In the role that I am in now, our sense of belonging data, according to the Panorama survey … was very low. And when I say low, it was below the 40th and 50th percentile level … So, when I saw that, I wanted to create a climate and create a culture where students see themselves, where students believed that they were valued, where students believed that they were connected to an adult. With that, when we gave the Panorama survey this past fall, guess what? Our sense of belonging data increased 11 percent."

When we allow room for mistakes, practice acceptance, value input from the most marginalized, actively share power, and embrace our communal diversity and strengths, we create spaces where all students are engaged, hopeful, feel a sense of belonging, and understand how to manage their emotions. Yes—these are all the factors mentioned by Gallup as important for student success. The strengths and assets of our school communities are already present. We need to remove the barriers that aren't allowing them to thrive.

WHAT YOU CAN DO TOMORROW

Now that we have presented our reframe for a strength-based community, you may need to better understand what we can do as individuals to strive toward these changes. How do we shatter our deficit beliefs that block our ability to look beyond traditional solutions to promote this real and meaningful change? Here are strategies you can adopt right away in your classrooms:

- **Start every day for a week with mindfulness meditation.** We can use many free resources and prompts in our classrooms or implement them during morning announcements to aid in beginning the day on a mindful note. See if behaviors change. Encourage your coworkers to do the same!

- **Try to sit at your desk as little as possible.** Walk around the room. Sit at tables with your students. Transform the power in your room through physicality. Encourage your coworkers to do the same!

- **Call the parent of a struggling student to celebrate something specific about the learner.** Challenge yourself to call one parent every week to talk about something positive. Be sure to garner feedback from them as well. Encourage your coworkers to do the same!

- **Talk less, smile more.** Challenge yourself to not talk for longer than ten to fifteen minutes in your classroom without pausing to check in with your students or switch to a more interactive activity. Also, remember how important nonverbal communication and gestures are in how we show support and appreciation for our students' involvement in their learning.

- **Seek questions over answers.** Drive your best learning by questioning students, which is especially essential in the younger years. Rather than focusing on a "right" answer, take questions from students seriously, even if they lead in a completely different direction than you intended. When students ask questions, they're engaged, and the wheels turn in their brains. We need to build upon that and encourage such inquiry.

When students ask unexpected questions, challenge yourself to broach these questions to the rest of the class by saying, "What does everyone think about this?" While it may not seem relevant to you or the curriculum, these are the authentic questions our students are curious about. Cain shares the following example, "So, you're teaching chemistry, and you're focusing on bonds, right? But they want to talk about melanin and how melanin changes because they look around the school and say, 'We have different melanin, is that a chemical thing?' Cool. So a student gets up and has that conversation."

- **Circle up!** Work on normalizing nontraditional seating arrangements that don't involve students in rows listening to a lecture. When we reshape our classroom (or staff meeting) into a circle, we automatically promote a sense of community and naturally engage everyone in the learning experience. They also transform power, allowing every participant to find their voice and engage in non-hierarchical learning.

- **Value feedback over grades.** There are likely many opportunities to reduce your reliance on grades in class. Challenge yourself to stop grading homework or traditional measures of participation. Instead, homework should focus on practicing new skills with the goal of low-stakes work. In terms of participation, bias and deficit thinking often limit how we allow participation, especially for students with unvalued cultural communication styles. Allow late work, redos, and retakes to serve as more useful student knowledge and growth measures. Tucker says, "When a student is struggling, don't assume the student needs to be tested for special education. Instead, talk with the student and family." Allow your students opportunities to share what is happening, what they need, and how best to support them without punishing them or assuming a disability.

You can use the following strategies at the school level:

- **Start a team meeting with a quote from a misunderstood student.** This could be a student who has been deemed a "problem" by most staff at school. Let this one quote guide your entire meeting and see how it goes. Assign one team member as the "anti-deficit police" who plays a sound whenever someone states a deficit belief or assumption. See if you can come up with some follow-up questions to ask the student when you see them next. See if you can identify potential schoolwide patterns from what this student has said.

- **Invite historically minoritized students to observe your staff meetings.** See what this accountability feels like. Hold a debriefing session and note what students observed.

- **Administer a brief student or parent survey.** Keep the survey broad and positive. Simply ask them what they enjoy about the school. Ask them what their favorite way to learn is. Disaggregate your data. Examine your practices and see what can be changed.

A BLUEPRINT FOR FULL IMPLEMENTATION

The only way we can dismantle the White supremacist notions that confine our ability to observe the community strengths of our schools is to reinvent the wheel. Everything we have introduced about disrupting deficit thinking at the school level comes down to trust—systems that value student voice, appreciate the strength of diversity, and practice vulnerability and accountability. This is why the full implementation of this practice seeks to develop cultures of trust and voice through social justice pedagogy by relying on the work of Safir and Dugan.

Step 1: Establish a staff-level community.

Before our students can feel a sense of community in our schools, we must feel it ourselves. If we don't feel safe and accepted in our schools, our students won't either. This has to start at the top, with administrators who value positive cultures. Rather than monthly staff meetings that involve reviewing administrative procedures, we need to allow for interactive and authentic experiences that lead to shared vulnerability and trust. We need to feel as if we can make mistakes without reprimand, that we can ask for help if we need it, and that there is no "dumb" question. This can only happen in spaces that take the time to value every staff member in the community, from the custodians to the principal.

Step 2: Create a shared mission, vision, and language.

Once you establish a sense of community, all community members can develop and agree on shared goals. All members of the community should play a role in reaching this vision. Ideally, the vision focuses on educators' roles in developing students' academic and social well-being. What is our vision of student success? What does it look like? How can we inclusively maintain high expectations for all students?

Step 3: Cultivate safe classroom communities.

Our classrooms must be spaces where students feel supported, respected, and challenged. Challenge yourself to engage in rituals such as check-ins, check-outs, restorative circles, and the sharing of roses and thorns. These are great opportunities to remind our students that there is no one reality, and we all bring different ideas into our community. Always assume a positive intent from our students. When we show our students that we believe in them, trust them to make good decisions, and value their feelings, we allow for a strong foundation when problems inevitably arise. When we start with love and respect, we receive it in return.

Step 4: Know your students.

Find out what your students know, what they're passionate about, and what assets and perspectives they bring to your room. What are their experiences, shared and different? What do they care about? What do they think? Implement activities that allow students to share their favorite foods, interests, sports, and more. Encourage activities that simultaneously teach you and them how they learn best, what their goals are, and what they need to be successful. Learn about their needs and provide them with choices about how and what they learn. Consider launching a storytime where students can volunteer to share their stories with you and the class. Get creative with ways to get to know your students as whole and vibrant people rather than information consumers.

Step 5: Develop your students as human beings *and* intellectuals.

We cannot continue to separate the act of academic learning from social-emotional learning. Tucker says, "The soul and the heart is a part of the learning just as much as the brain."

We must aim to understand who our students are, where they come from, and what familial strengths they bring into our schools. Our teaching styles and approaches will always serve as models for students. Model vulnerability and embrace mistakes and imperfections. Show your students that you respect their thoughts, feelings, and ideas. Set boundaries for and with your students. Be an ally for their holistic needs. Treat them as sources of knowledge and refrain from the notion that there is only one right answer. Allow your classroom to serve as a community of inquiry, accountability, and respect for other people's ideas.

Step 6: Let students do the work.

Once students know how they learn best, we can teach them how to use those strengths and advocate for learning opportunities where they can thrive. Teachers should serve as coaches, supporting students in navigating individual and community needs. Differentiation can occur without tracking when students know what they need, why they need it, and how to access it. An example involves providing multiple stations with varying levels of support and encouraging students to choose which station *they* feel they need to be successful. Allow your students opportunities to teach how they came to certain conclusions and what tasks were more difficult or easier for them. Encourage students to take turns developing the learning goals for the day and taking ownership in holding themselves and their classmates accountable for reaching those goals.

Step 7: Ground curriculum in student realities.

Teach from a curriculum grounded in social justice to help students understand and navigate the real world. Every activity in our schools must have a clear and relevant purpose. Encourage critical thinking, acknowledge and address conflict, and allow for healthy debates.

Step 8: Incorporate HUMANE data collection throughout this process.

Most importantly, continue to garner feedback from students about what's working and what's not working. Each of us can work harder to be open to criticism and opportunities to change.

OVERCOMING PUSHBACK

When we talk about school-level practices, it's fair to feel overwhelmed. With so many areas out of your control, you may feel powerless to adopt the changes you believe will make a difference. Catch yourself in these moments and refocus your energy to where you do have control. Following are a few ways this may manifest within you, along with ways to regain your control and reframe your beliefs about this approach.

My standardized curriculum and testing schedules don't allow for this flexibility. This is often the biggest barrier to creativity in the classroom. However, we can still co-create collaborative spaces when we practice vulnerability with ourselves and our students. Be real with students about factors out of your control—namely, standardized testing. However, we challenge you to truly think about how you can meet the learning objectives in ways that don't diminish our students' sense of agency and purpose.

My administrators are not on board with this approach. One cannot undermine the importance of having administrators who bring an inclusive and welcoming approach into our building. When we don't have that, it is extremely difficult to make an impact at the school level. We challenge you to identify at least one other individual in the building who is interested in a strength-based approach. Focus on what you can do together and consider advocating for change together. School districts can get very political very fast, and it is always tricky to navigate the complex relationships at play. However, when we ground our approaches and ideas in the needs of students, it is always possible to find common ground with people who don't agree.

If I give up my power, the students will be out of control. We are led to believe that adults know all, and children will take advantage of us if we loosen the reins. Our culture of individualism or perfectionism tells us that if we want something done correctly, we need to do it ourselves. However, you'd be surprised by the combination of leveraging power paired with a strong community. When students respect themselves, their learning, and you, they will prove this belief wrong. Just as adults prefer to have input into their experiences, children crave opportunities to have a say in what their learning looks like. The more power we give our students, the more motivation and buy-in they will have. We also need to unpack what "out of control" means. What may appear "out of control" to us could actually be a meaningful learning experience for our students. Challenge yourself.

THE REFRAME IN ACTION

Mr. Johnson is a tenth grade English teacher who has been in the field for twenty years. In the beginning of a new school year, he was past burnout but wanted to see what would happen when he attempted a pedagogy of voice and trust within his classroom. He'd previously been a leader in the school; however, a new principal in the building had begun undermining his ideas. Thus, he decided that all he could do at this point was focus on the culture of his class. He saw four blocks of tenth graders twice daily, so he reminded himself that he could impact all students in tenth grade if he put his mind to it.

Johnson decided that his goal for the year was to develop student autonomy. This goal was in addition to the common core standards he knew he must ensure his students meet. Johnson dedicated the first week of school to developing shared norms with each of his classes and getting to know his students personally. He did so in a circle format where students were encouraged to share more about themselves, what school means to them, and their future goals. He opened up each first circle with vulnerability, sharing that this was his first time attempting a circle format. He shared that he didn't have a positive experience when he was in school until one teacher changed his trajectory in eleventh grade. He realized that his vulnerability allowed students to feel comfortable doing the same. He learned about many of their experiences up until that point and that many of them had not had positive experiences. They discussed what went wrong, what worked well, and what they envisioned for the current school year. He ended each period by encouraging students to submit an anonymous exit slip where they could reflect on the day's lesson and provide feedback or criticism. By the end of the week, he found that his students clearly understood the goals for both courses. He felt satisfied by the mostly positive feedback he received.

Johnson next implemented a learning-style quiz where students figured out what type of learners they were. He asked them if they wanted to chat with other people who learn the same way or with people who learn differently. He found it interesting that each of his blocks collectively chose different things.

In one block, the students wanted to talk to both. In another block, the students had the great idea to present their learning styles in the format they learn best. The group of visual learners created a presentation, the group of auditory learners lectured, and the group of interactive learners implemented an activity. Then Johnson laughed with the students about how each presentation was different than what the audience preferred. He took it upon himself to use that experience as an example of what lack of inclusion feels like. A student in one block mentioned a book that also demonstrated inclusion specific to neurodiversity. Johnson decided to let the students choose if they wanted to read that book or another book to start the year.

He was amazed at how enthusiastic his students had become when he treated them with respect and dignity. While he expected his students to have too much freedom, making them difficult to control, he reminded himself that his goal was not to control them but to develop their autonomy. Johnson continued the rest of the year with a flexible approach, allowing a new student to choose a central theme each time and allowing the rest of the students to choose which book they ultimately wanted to read. The themes were grounded in student reality—inclusion, advocacy, democracy, multiculturalism, and justice. He noticed a significant difference in the discussions when students read (or listened to) books of interest. Johnson did not assign homework, but he encouraged them to read at home. While he did assign grades, he always allowed students multiple opportunities to demonstrate their knowledge. He did not accept subpar material. Rather than assigning a grade and moving on, he met with each student biweekly for about five minutes. They reviewed how they were doing, their feelings, and what they needed.

He challenged his students to think of thought-provoking questions about what they were reading, and he had volunteers facilitate discussions. He allowed students to demonstrate their knowledge and understanding in any way they wanted—as long as he approved it. He was surprised to see the creative genius in his students as they created raps, read poems, painted elaborate portraits, engaged in role-play, designed complex digital graphics, and presented edited videos to reflect their knowledge. Students were engaged and interested in the different ways their classmates contributed to the environment. Johnson didn't require assigned seats this year, and he realized that students were sitting with different people throughout the year rather than situating themselves in one space and with one group.

While Johnson continued his HUMANE data collection with students, he also garnered input from parents. When students seemed off, he simply asked them what they needed. He'd never seen such openness from high school students. Because Johnson happened to be on cycle this year, the new principal would observe his instruction. After his observation, he was worried the principal would reprimand him for his unstructured approach. However, Johnson was surprised that the administration acknowledged him at the next staff meeting for his new, innovative approach. At the end of the year, Johnson joined the leadership team because the principal was interested in adopting his approaches at the school level for the following year.

We know this work is not easy. We know it is not straightforward. We know it takes honest reflection and strength. But we encourage you to remember what we have control over. The environment we exist in impacts how we feel, how we move, and how we choose to navigate it. What changes can you make to allow your students to navigate our systems with authenticity?

EDUCATORS DESERVE TO FLOURISH
Finally Flourishing

The time has come for a new prosperity, one that takes flourishing seriously as the goal of education and of parenting. Learning to value and to attain flourishing must start early— in the formative years of schooling—and it is this new prosperity, kindled by positive education, that the world can now choose.

— MARTIN SELIGMAN, FOUNDER OF POSITIVE PSYCHOLOGY

THE BELIEF:
EDUCATORS NEVER PROSPER

ONE OF THE most detrimental outcomes of deficit thinking is its impact on our belief that we are powerless. Again— because deficit thinking blames our students and families for problems, we are left with the belief that the work we do as educators will never be enough. So often, educators are blamed for students misbehaving, not meeting grade-level standards, or not living up to some unrealistic goal. These often-unattainable standards lead to educator burnout: stress, anxiety, depression, fatigue, guilt, sorrow, feelings of inadequacy, shame, and doubt.

We have seen a mass exodus of teachers leaving education in recent years, often referred to as the great resignation. Educators are leaving the field in record numbers because they are burned out.

We consider burnout to be no different than clinical manifestations of mental illness. When educators feel burned out, they report feeling like there was nothing else they could do and they could no longer make a difference. Remember that our schools are designed to lead you to believe that you can't make a difference. Yet, you can make a difference.

Educators deserve to prosper and to experience joy. You deserve to be happy, lead a satisfying life, come to work happy, be content, feel respected and valued, be part of a team, and know your work makes a difference. Sadly, this isn't always the case, and this has to change with lightning speed. In this Reframe, we introduce and build on the work from Seligman and Peterson and introduce a new prosperity—flourishing.

THE REFRAME:
EDUCATORS DESERVE TO FLOURISH

When educators flourish, health, productivity, and peace follow.

We have frequently discussed Martin Seligman and Chris Peterson throughout this book. Both are influential in the field of Positive Psychology. Seligman says he used to think Positive Psychology was about happiness, the gold standard for measuring happiness was life satisfaction, and the goal of Positive Psychology was to increase life satisfaction.

Seligman went through a massive shift in his belief about the field. He asked the question, "What makes life worth living?"

Some might say all human behavior is to achieve happiness. Others might say it is to avoid pain, anxiety, and misery. Seligman and his team spent years surveying thousands of people, researching, and conducting studies to answer the question of what made life worth living.

Eventually, he arrived at the belief that the aspect that made life worth living is the construct of well-being. Therefore, he based the focus of Positive Psychology on well-being. Further, the goal of Positive Psychology is to increase flourishing. In short, he found that people want meaning and purpose in life.

Seligman and his team's work is rooted in scientific evidence, and it is grounded in the same tried-and-true methods people use in measurement and experiments:

- It uses longitudinal research, which includes repeated studies on the same participants over time.

- It is randomly assigned. Some groups use a new method, and some don't. No one in the experiment (including the experimenters) knows who belongs in which group.

- It's placebo-controlled, meaning some students and researchers believe they are using a new strategy even though they're not. Researchers compared the group with the treatment to the people who did not receive it to see if there was a difference. (Does it really work, or do people simply believe they're doing better because they tried to do *something*?)

It discards ineffective interventions and hones the ones that work. Seligman found that the old gold standard of Positive Psychology tied too closely to mood. The new standard of Positive Psychology has five elements of well-being:

- Positive emotion
- Engagement

- Positive relationships

- Meaning

- Achievement

Because using your strengths leads to more positive emotion, more meaning, more accomplishment, and better relationships, they are the basis of well-being. You might think that living well would be about having lots of money or being able to buy whatever you want whenever you want. But the truth is that's not what life is all about. Living well is about flourishing. To us, flourishing is about feeling good, finding joy in your work, having meaning and fulfilling relationships, and having a sense of accomplishment. Despite your circumstances, you have the power to choose your course in life by maximizing all five.

The goal of Positive Psychology, then, is to help people flourish. If you want to flourish and increase your well-being, you must minimize your misery. Seligman shared how he, as a therapist, would help clients get rid of anger, anxiety, and sadness. He thought they would become happier people—but they never did. Instead, his patients felt empty because they lacked flourishing skills such as:

- Positive emotions

- Meaning

- Good work

- Positive relationships

WHAT YOU CAN DO TOMORROW

Seligman recognized that the skills needed to flourish are above and beyond the skills needed to minimize suffering. Initially, he only had the tools for relieving depression. But every person, every patient, wants to be happy, relieve suffering, and build well-being.

- **Learn and be able to describe the PERMA model.** The PERMA model represents the five primary elements of happiness and well-being. It stands for Positive emotion, Engagement, Relationships, Meaning, and Accomplishments. Everyone benefits from learning the skills of Positive Psychology.

- **Communicate the need for these skills.** Students need to learn these specific skills to help them flourish. These skills of flourishing reduce depression and anxiety and likely help prevent them as well. Seligman identified an evidence-based way to create more positive emotions, greater meaning, stronger accomplishments, and better relationships. He believed that all schools at every level should teach these skills of well-being.

- **Find ways to create and experience more positive emotions.** We can increase our positive emotions about the past (e.g., by cultivating gratitude and forgiveness), our positive emotions about the present (e.g., by savoring physical pleasures and mindfulness), and our positive emotions about the future (e.g., by building hope and optimism). This route to well-being may be limited by how much an individual can experience positive emotions. In other words, positive affectivity is partly heritable, and our emotions tend to fluctuate within a range. Many people are, by disposition, less likely to experience positive emotions. Traditional conceptions of happiness tend to focus on positive emotions, so it can be liberating to know that there are other routes to well-being.

- **Fully engage in an activity.** Engagement is an experience where someone fully uses their skills, strengths, and attention for an activity. According to psychologist Mihaly Csikszentmihalyi, this produces an experience called "flow" that is so gratifying that people are willing to do it for its own sake instead of what they will get out of it. The activity is its own reward. We experience flow when we have enough skills to meet challenges to pursue a clear goal, and we have immediate feedback on our progress. In such an activity, concentration is fully absorbed at the moment, self-awareness disappears, and the perception of time is distorted in retrospect (time seems to have stopped). We can experience flow in a wide variety of activities, such as:

  ▸ Good conversations

  ▸ Work tasks

  ▸ Playing a musical instrument

  ▸ Reading a book

- ‣ Writing
- ‣ Building furniture
- ‣ Fixing a bike
- ‣ Gardening
- ‣ Sports training
- ‣ Performances

- **Prioritize positive relationships.** The experiences that contribute to well-being are often amplified through our relationships. These moments of well-being include great joy, meaning, laughter, a feeling of belonging, and pride in accomplishment. Connections to others can give life purpose and meaning and serve as one of the best antidotes to "the downs" of life. From an evolutionary perspective, we are social beings because the drive to connect with and serve others promotes our survival. Developing strong relationships is central to adaptation and is enabled by our capacity for love, compassion, kindness, empathy, teamwork, cooperation, and self-sacrifice.

  Seek more meaning in life. You will gain a sense of meaning and purpose when you serve something bigger than the self. Social institutions can give a sense of meaning, including family, science, politics, religion, work organizations, justice, the community, and social causes.

A BLUEPRINT FOR FULL IMPLEMENTATION

In this section, we begin by providing a blueprint to help you take actionable steps to name, know, and use your strengths. The following blueprint will help you understand your thinking, shift away from deficit thinking, and move toward owning your strengths. We believe the steps you take toward naming, knowing, and using your strengths will underpin each area of well-being in your life. Finally, this blueprint will help you figure out your strengths and how they contribute to your level of flourishing.

Step 1: Identify your strengths.

Before you can understand your strengths, first name your strengths. One way to name your strengths is to take an assessment. Here are three assessments we recommend to identify and name your strengths.

CliftonStrengths Assessment. The CliftonStrengths Assessment is an online assessment to help you identify and begin to understand your strengths. The assessment typically takes anywhere from thirty to sixty minutes to complete. It has paired statements and you select which statement describes you the best. The CliftonStrengths Assessment will help you discover what you naturally do best by measuring your natural patterns of how you think, feel, and behave in various situations. The best part about the CliftonStrengths Assessment is that it names your top five strengths, and this is a valuable and memorable part of the results.

Perhaps the only drawback is a nominal fee associated with the assessment. You will also have to pay more if you want access to the full results (top thirty-four themes, not just your top five). While it does cost, we like this assessment because it provides you with a comprehensive and customized report containing the detailed results of your assessment.

Enneagram Assessment. The Enneagram is one of the most popular systems for classifying personality types. It is a strength-based assessment and provides nine different personality types within the Enneagram theory divided by Heart Types, Head Types, and Body Types. People with Heart Types generally rely more on emotional intelligence to understand their reactions and connect with others. Head Types are bright and inquisitive people who enjoy making sense of the world and figuring out how things work. They communicate through facts and data, so they want you to put your message in logical and rational terms. People who fall into the Body Type domain typically rely on their intuitive intelligence rather than rational intelligence to guide them.

Each personality type is defined by a particular core belief about the world and how it works. The Enneagram offers self-knowledge and personal development to better understand one's core motivations and apply that knowledge to all areas of life, including conflict resolution, team dynamics, leadership, and emotional intelligence. The Enneagram helps to identify areas of growth for personal and professional development. Perhaps the best part about the Enneagram is that you can take this assessment for free.

Values in Action (VIA) Character Strengths Survey. As mentioned in an earlier Reframe, the fields of education and psychology have focused primarily on pathology and identifying what's wrong with people. Assessment practices, especially within psychology, focused almost exclusively on treating mental illness. Along with Martin Seligman, who is widely held as the creator of the field of Positive Psychology, Chris Peterson strived to identify what's right with people. Seligman and a team of researchers and scientists began their study of strengths in the early 2000s when scientists attempted to study character more scientifically. Their findings developed the VIA Classification of Character Strengths and Virtues, a classification of positive traits in human beings. Since then, hundreds of peer-reviewed articles have been published across many cultures.

The VIA Survey measures twenty-four character strengths in individuals. Seligman and Peterson believe we all possess these character strengths and link them to personal growth, well-being, and life satisfaction. We love the VIA because it's free, has been widely researched and validated, and offers a survey for children called the VIA Youth Survey. The VIA Youth Survey was adapted from the original version and designed for youth between ten and seventeen years old.

Step 2: Ask a friend or colleague to describe your strengths.

If you don't like taking assessments or don't want to pay to find out about your strengths, then asking someone close to you might be a useful way to better understand your strengths. Get started by asking friends, family, loved ones, or colleagues what they think your strengths are. This is a useful method, especially if it is challenging for you to be introspective personally.

You might also consider feedback from a superior or school leader. Many schools or companies have regularly scheduled performance reviews and evaluations. If you have a healthy relationship with your superior or school leader, and if they conduct performance reviews objectively and fairly, then it might be worth considering those strengths.

Step 3: Understand your strengths.

Once you can name your strengths, you can begin to understand those strengths to give you a sense of purpose. Say that one of your top CliftonStrengths is *relator*. Relators thrive on relationships, get along well with others, and find satisfaction in working as part of a team to reach a goal. Imagine that a relator has been frustrated in a job because they work alone and in isolation. A person who doesn't understand that relators thrive in relationships and teams will struggle in a job that isolates and doesn't involve collaboration. However, a relator will most likely thrive and find meaning when put in a position to work with others, collaborate, and navigate social settings that might otherwise be difficult for non-relators. Simply put, when you can name and then understand your strengths, you can put yourself in situations (or possibly even remove yourself) where you are more likely (or unlikely) to find success and thrive.

If you don't know your strengths, how can you express the amazing things you know you can do? How can you know what potential roles and responsibilities fit with who you are and what you love? How can you lead others in a way that aligns with your strengths if you don't know what they are? How can you help students succeed using their strengths if you don't know your own? Knowing your strengths is essential to knowing who you are and where your abilities lie. It's the rich soil out of which the tree of your life grows.

Reflect on your top strengths and how you have used them in your life. Here are a few excellent questions to help you reflect and better understand your strengths:

- What has given you the most energy in your life?
- What are the earliest memories you have of your strengths?
- Who were you before the world told you who to be?
- When, if ever, have your strengths gone dark? Why?
- Name one strength and how you can begin using it more often.

When you can understand your strengths, you can move from a position of simply surviving to thriving in your life. You deserve to thrive. You deserve to know your top strengths, what those strengths mean, and how best to put those strengths into action.

Step 4: Apply your strengths to make an immediate impact.

Once you have taken a strength-based assessment and can name your top strengths—you are ready to begin using and applying your strengths to make an immediate impact. Here are a few ways to begin applying your strengths.

> **Share your strengths.** Have you ever been looked over for a job or task you know you would've been great at? One reason could simply be because someone is unaware of your strengths. Imagine that one of your top CliftonStrengths is *strategic*. Strategic people are exceptional at recognizing patterns, navigating hurdles, and accomplishing goals because they know where they should start and can create a plan through to the finish line.
>
> In a workplace, strategic people might be more introverted, risk-averse, and exceptional at recognizing potential pitfalls or gaps in plans. Even more, strategic people have difficulty functioning when there isn't a plan. Those who aren't strategic as a strength might perceive non-strategic individuals as problematic, not being team players, or combative. Knowing the strengths of each member in a group can help teams and organizations proactively leverage their strengths. The bottom line is to be proactive with your strengths and realize it's okay to set the tone for how you use them.

Write a personal mission statement using your strengths. Just as organizations and companies create mission statements to guide their decisions and inform their internal teams and external audiences about their purpose, you can develop a personal mission statement to guide your decisions and share your intent. Your mission statement can describe what you hope to accomplish simply and concisely. Once you know your strengths, you can align your strengths with your purpose by working them into your mission statement.

Take the PERMA assessments and reflect on results. The Authentic Happiness website developed by Seligman's team at the University of Pennsylvania offers a variety of assessments and surveys through their questionnaire center. The website offers three tools you can use for free to measure flourishing: the PERMA Survey, which measures your five aspects of flourishing; the PERMA Meter, a quick assessment; and the Workplace PERMA Profile to help you determine how much you're flourishing at work. When you're done, review and reflect on your results. What areas are you flourishing in? In what areas would you like to flourish more? These questions will help you take action to increase your flourishing.

Step 5: Choose a flourishing activity.

The good news is that each one of us can increase our level of flourishing, happiness, and well-being. Saying thank you to someone, whether through a note, a call, or face to face, will increase your level of flourishing. Practice the Three Good Things activity in Reframe 6. Every night before you go to sleep, think of Three Good Things that happened to you and write them down. Reflect on your role in why those good things happened so you can generate even more good things.

OVERCOMING PUSHBACK

Some people will try to persuade you to view the world through a deficit lens, but now you know that's a limiting belief. You deserve to flourish, and so do your students. Here are a few areas of pushback you may encounter.

Mental illness is too complicated to be fixed by well-being efforts. Many people struggle with clinically significant levels of stress, anxiety, and depression and may need treatment, therapy, or drugs to help ease their symptoms. While well-being efforts are not a cure, they are beneficial to everyone. Educators, especially, are in a visible position to model well-being and help their students gain well-being skills for life.

I'm just getting through my day and don't have time to add well-being activities. You don't have time not to focus on your well-being! Well-being deeply connects to our overall health, productivity, ability to work well with others, and the quality of our relationships. It's also linked to physical factors like blood pressure, immune function, and cardiovascular function. In a study published by the American Psychological Association, researchers from the University of Pennsylvania examined 2,765 participants between eighteen and sixty-eight. The study found that individuals with higher levels of well-being were more cooperative, had stronger immune systems, and performed better at work than their counterparts with lower levels of well-being. In addition, they were more prosocial, had fewer sleep problems and less burnout, and reported better physical health than people with lower levels of well-being. Those with higher levels of well-being tended to be less materialistic and more satisfied with life overall.

Teachers should only work for the love of kids. Teachers, educators, and school leaders have all made a conscious decision to work with children. Perhaps they felt love and passion for working with young people and helping to shape the future. Perhaps doing this work contributes to their sense of well-being! Our work matters, and each one of us as individuals matters. We deserve to answer the questions: "What makes life worth living?" and "How can I focus on my strengths and flourish?"

THE REFRAME IN ACTION

Ms. Overton was at her wit's end. As she sat in the office with her school's principal and vice-principal, she expressed frustration. For starters, she had worked at the school for a decade. She was a staple in the community with excellent relationships with students, parents, coworkers, and the community. Despite her longevity in the school and community, she no longer felt valued. The school forced her to switch grade levels at the start of the year without asking for her input. She struggled to receive the support she needed from her school leadership.

Personally, Overton had recently gone through a divorce. She went from living in a single-family home to an apartment with her two young children. She expressed to her administration that her rent had just gone up, and she hadn't received a cost-of-living adjustment in years. Because of the discrepancy between the increasing rate and lack of salary increase, she might soon be priced out of her apartment. Because of her professional and personal challenges, she was struggling.

Overton began therapy for the challenges she was experiencing. Her first homework assignment in therapy was the Three Good Things activity. The therapist tasked her with reflecting on Three Good Things that happened and why. At the end of each day for a week, she reflected on Three Good Things that happened to her. By the middle of the week, she started to notice a shift. She felt that she started intentionally searching for positive moments throughout the day so she might document them later on. By actively searching for positive moments, she noticed her demeanor improved. Perhaps it's the law of attraction. Maybe it's the idea that you find more of what you're actively searching for. Whatever the reason, Overton was locked into looking for positives instead of negatives.

> **If you want to thrive, you have to understand your strengths and then use them to increase your well-being. You deserve to flourish.**

By the end of the week, she decided to make this activity part of her daily routine. She shared that she felt less overwhelmed and more optimistic. Interestingly, Overton reported that she let go of those things outside of her control. She experienced more positive emotions, felt less overwhelmed, lowered her stress, and was generally happier and felt more in control of herself and her attitudes as she navigated the challenges in her personal and professional life.

We've learned to identify the worst in people. By adopting that logic, we ignore the innate human potential. Instead, let's leverage our strengths to unlock our potential. Once you understand your strengths, you can apply them in your personal and professional endeavors and make a big difference in how you live your life. If you want to thrive, you have to understand your strengths and then use them to increase your well-being. You deserve to flourish. You are worthy of living a meaningful life. Your well-being matters. That is how you shift from what's wrong to what's strong.

CONCLUSION
Wrapping Up

WHEN WE ACTIVELY take the time to understand where deficit thinking stems from and how it operates within our minds and classrooms today, we can begin to embark on a path of flourishing. Our perception dictates so much of how we interact with the world. Actively cultivating asset-based perceptions of all students, especially those at the margins, allows us to regain control over our actions to reimagine the purpose of education.

When we disrupt deficit thinking in our schools and release its hold over our actions, we rid ourselves of the blame-based shackles that produce and reinforce inequities in student outcomes. Let's ensure that we give all our students every opportunity to succeed. We can help them understand their strengths and realize it is a continual process of actualizing who they are and what they hope to become. It's a way of making sense of the world around us and answering the deep philosophical question—who am I? By understanding our strengths, we can lead more satisfying, fulfilling, and meaningful lives.

In conclusion, we offer the following words of wisdom and encouragement from our incredibly brilliant contributors.

"If we can change just one piece of what we do through the thinking that we have, then we're on the road to healing."
— Nikole Hollins-Sims

"Everybody has somebody that they care about, everybody has something that they love, and when we allow students the opportunity to share those things with us, it helps us to see them in a different light."
— Ashley Tucker

"When we [adopt] an asset-based frame of mind, oftentimes our whole energy, our whole approach, changes so systemically."
— Nikole Hollins-Sims

"Get vulnerable and start with yourself, be gracious with yourself while you are learning and transforming, and take the time to listen."
— Krista Rice

"Speak up and out. Cultivate positive and meaningful relationships in your system so you can talk about and suggest reform on deficit thinking."
— Wendy Turner

"Our educational system is overly taxed right now, but it has such rich potential, and therefore we need to harness the really good individuals, the really good systems and supports in schools, to grow the strength of school systems and communities to achieve even higher and stronger outcomes for all students— not just some, for all."
— Tim Runge

"If the system says it can't happen, change the system. You and your students can and should be whoever you want to be."
— Richard Williams

APPENDIX

Example questions your team may consider during the "Unpack" phase of HUMANE data collection (see Reframe 3).

Highlight your satellite data: We've seen a rise in attendance concerns and tardiness.

*Questions to **unpack:***

- What is our process for documenting attendance/tardies?

- Are all teachers following the same attendance/tardy procedure?

- Have we changed our practices/routines/instruction in any way that could impact attendance?

- Are we lacking awareness about our community that would lead to increased absences/tardies during a specific time period (holidays, cultural traditions, etc.)?

- What do students think is the cause?

- What do parents think?

- Can students and parents suggest ways to reduce absences?

Highlight your satellite data: Black males are sent to the office more than White males.

*Questions to **unpack:***

- What behaviors lead to office referrals (per the code of conduct), and are they rooted in anti-racism?

- Do all staff have the same understanding of what these behaviors look like?

- Who is doing the referring? Is it an isolated or schoolwide concern?

- What strategies should staff attempt before referring students to the office?

- Are these strategies more likely to be attempted with White males? If so, have our Black males noticed, and why do they think they are being referred at higher rates?

- Are these strategies rooted in anti-racism?

- How do our Black males feel at school? Do we need to change our practices to make school a positive experience for them?

Highlight your satellite data: Students in one specific class are more likely to receive failing grades.

*Questions to **unpack**:*

- What do this teacher's instructional practices look like?

- What is the classroom's climate?

- What do the teacher-student relationships look like in this room?

- What classroom management techniques does this teacher use?

- What is teacher-parent communication like?

- What is this teacher's approach to grading?

- How have students performed in this classroom in previous years?

- Does the teacher feel like the students are learning?

- Do the students feel like they are learning?

- How do the students perceive this teacher?

Highlight your satellite data: Monolingual students perform better than EL students in math.

*Questions to **unpack:***

- What is the cultural loading (information only available to certain cultures) of our math curriculum?

- What is the verbal loading of our math curriculum?

- Are we implementing approaches and practices that are engaging for our EL students?

- What language is instruction presented in?

- Are our EL students receiving the same instruction as our monolingual students?

- What strategies are we providing to ensure our EL students have tools for success?

- How do our EL students feel about their math performance?

Highlight your satellite data: We see a significant number of office referrals during lunchtime.

*Questions to **unpack:***

- Who is in the cafeteria during lunchtime?

- What behaviors are considered worthy of a referral?

- What are the behavioral expectations during lunchtime? Do students and teachers have the same understanding of these expectations?

- Do we have enough adults to support the lunchtime needs of students?

- What can we do as a school to ensure students feel supported in the cafeteria?

- Do our students enjoy lunchtime?

- How do they feel at lunch?

Highlight your satellite data: More White students are in gifted education than students of color.

*Questions to **unpack:***

- What procedures do we use to refer students to gifted education, and are they rooted in anti-racism?

- Who is doing the referring?

- What methods are used to qualify students, and are they rooted in anti-racism?

- What practices can we implement that will naturally cultivate the strengths of our students of color and allow us to view them as worthy of gifted education?

- How knowledgeable are parents from diverse backgrounds about gifted education?

- How do our students of color feel about their schooling?

Highlight your satellite data: LGBTQ+ students self-refer to counseling more than straight/cisgender students.

*Questions to **unpack:***

- Is our culture a welcoming space for LGBTQ+ students?

- Do our LGBTQ+ students feel connected to the staff at school?

- Do they feel more comfortable with the school counselor? If so, why?

- Are there specific teachers who might be contributing to the influx?

- What biases might our school staff harbor about LGBTQ+ students?

- Are the referral concerns related to our school practices and procedures?

- What do we need to change about our school to ensure that LGBTQ+ students receive the emotional support they need from their classrooms?

Highlight your satellite data: White students receive more tiered support than Latinx students.

*Questions to **unpack:***

- What is our referral method for tiered supports, and are they rooted in anti-racism?

- What procedures are in place to either approve or deny a referral?

- Do we have unidentified Latinx students who also need additional support?

- Are we over-identifying White students?

- Is teacher bias playing a role in referrals?

- What do our Latinx students perceive to be the cause?

Highlight your satellite data: Our after-school program has low participation by Black students.

*Questions to **unpack:***

- What after-school programs are we offering?

- Are they of interest to our Black students?

- What type of culture or climate are we cultivating for our Black students?

- Do they feel welcome in our space?

- Do we know if they are interested in other after-school activities that we haven't thought of?

- Have we asked our Black students?

- Are there other barriers to participation we haven't thought of?

Highlight your satellite data: Amharic-speaking students are not progressing in the English language at the same rate as Spanish-speaking students.

*Questions to **unpack:***

- What do our EL/ESOL supports look like?

- What do our standardized assessments measure?

- Do we have any Amharic-speaking staff? If not, how can we bridge that gap?

- Are we missing a key cultural component in our approach?

- What do our Amharic students and communities think?

- Do they believe it is an accurate depiction of their English-speaking abilities?

SNEAK PEEK

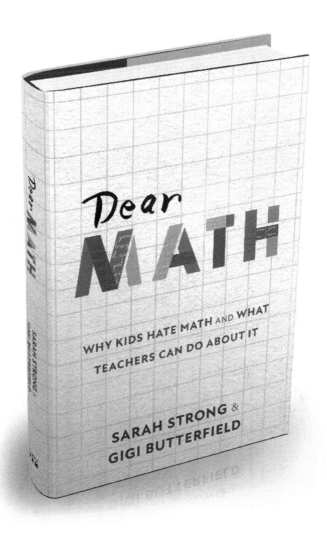

"**D**EAR MATH, I hate you; you make my clear skies feel gray. In a world without you, I don't know what I would do, though your own significance doesn't have to involve me. I've never liked your certainty of 'right' or 'wrong' when it ends up with just me unknowingly being dragged along."
—HAYLEY, TWELFTH GRADE

Because math invokes such strong emotions, often feelings associated with dislike and dread, I hope that we can hold space for these emotions and create activities where students can explicitly share their stories and unpack their feelings. Beyond caring about math and our students, we need to care about our math stories, particularly mathematical identities: how students see themselves as mathematicians and participate in mathematical spaces.

When he was president of the National Council of Teachers of Mathematics, Robert Berry stated, "Effective teachers affirm positive mathematical identities among all of their students, especially students of color."

But why should we care about our students' mathematical identities? Can't we just teach them the processes they need to know?

The answer to this is, as we will see throughout this book, an emphatic "No."

The learning process inherently includes the development of identity. In his book on communities of learners, Étienne Wenger (1998) explains, "Because learning transforms who we are and what we can do, it is an experience of identity. It is not just an accumulation of skills and information but a process of becoming—to become a certain person or, conversely, to avoid becoming a certain person. Even the learning that we do entirely by ourselves contributes to making us into a specific kind of person. We accumulate skills and information, not in the abstract as ends in themselves, but in the service of an identity."

Students naturally form their own mathematical identities with or without our involvement. If we want students to engage in a better relationship with math, we need to guide them toward more positive mathematical identities. Recognizing how the unpleasant feelings they already have affect their identities is a strong first step.

"Dear Math, You are a cruel, heartless mistress."

—TONY, TWELFTH GRADE

Being able to share such strong emotions clearly creates the space to forge a path out of these emotions. Students may not even need advice or solutions for the problems they are experiencing; they may just periodically need to vent. Students come into our classrooms each day with a great variety of stories. If we do not create space for them to share their stories, then we are making it more difficult to help them create healthier relationships with math overall.

A LESS DREADFUL EXPERIENCE

Dear Math letters are a critical tool for understanding and overcoming dread for two related reasons. The first reason is that the letters give students a space to share their story, vent, and unpack the ways they have become the mathematician they are today. We can normalize experiences from the past, process them, and collectively make sense of a path forward.

The second reason comes from the teaching standpoint. If we don't ask, then we are designing curricula and making instructional decisions by relying on our assumptions from prior experiences, our own math experiences, or feedback we get from the loudest students.

I used to follow the ignorance-is-bliss concept, ignoring how my students already felt in favor of making my class as awesome as possible to help them love math. How wrong I was. I regularly assumed that the students were as ready to think about math as I was and that they were excited to learn it in the same ways that had excited me. I am reminded of Chimamanda Adichie's famous 2009 TED Talk entitled "The Danger of a Single Story."

In it, she states, "The single story creates stereotypes, and the problem with stereotypes is not that they are untrue but that they are incomplete. They make one story become the only story."

"Dear Math, I have always hated you; I can never do you. Sometimes I get the answer, but that's only on the better types of math. But I guess I need you because those 'Sometimes' are important in daily life. But I still hate you. I never look forward to doing you, I always look forward to finishing you and going on with my day."

— SAM, TENTH GRADE

Mathematics classrooms are easy spaces to become "one story." There is a math problem, there is a way to solve it, everyone tries it and does well or doesn't, and then we move on to the next problem. Dear Math letters hold space for and give voice to all the different math stories in the room. They allow healing for those with traumatic math stories and encourage the co-creation of stories that are whole and complete. Most importantly, they tell us things we wouldn't have known if we hadn't asked.

Every time I open a new Google Drive folder containing my students' Dear Math letters, my heart starts beating a little faster. I know some letters will reveal a dread for the subject that I must engage students in each day for an entire semester. I'll have to address their feelings in the ways that I teach. If the dread that students feel is connected to feeling rushed, we might try out fewer activities in our class that focus on speed. If their dread is connected to their grades, we might consider alternative grading activities or more equity-oriented assessment strategies.

But if I didn't ask, then I might delude myself into thinking that everyone was walking into my class ready to have a good time. Furthermore, I might unintentionally impose my own math story and identity markers onto my students, joining the oppressive figures I sought to dispel. Delusion and oppression are unhealthy starting places for a semester of work together.

BUY *DEAR MATH*

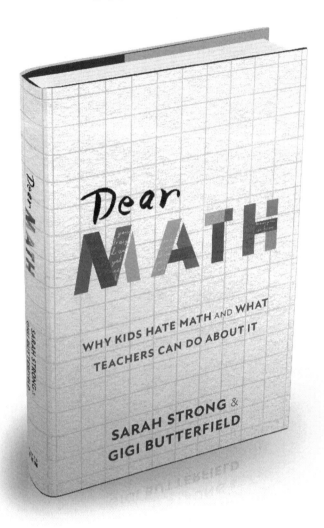

AVAILABLE AT:
Amazon.com
10Publications.com
and bookstores near you

ABOUT THE AUTHORS

Byron McClure

Dr. Byron McClure, D.Ed., is a nationally certified school psychologist and founder of Lessons For SEL. He uses research and human-centered design thinking to build empathy, ideate, co-create solutions, and design equitable resources that put the needs of people front and center. While formerly serving as the assistant director of school redesign at a high school in Southeast Washington, DC, he reimagined social-emotional learning within an inner-city community. His work centers on influencing systemic change and ensuring students from high-poverty communities have access to a quality education.

Dr. McClure has extensive knowledge and expertise in mental health, social-emotional learning, and behavior. He has done considerable work advocating for fair and equitable discipline practices for all students, particularly for African American boys. He has designed and implemented school-wide initiatives such as SEL, restorative practices, MTSS, and trauma-responsive practices. Dr. McClure has presented as a panelist, featured speaker, and keynote speaker across the country. He believes in shifting from what's wrong to what's strong. Follow him on Twitter @schoolpsychlife and Instagram @bmcclure6.

Kelsie Reed

Dr. Kelsie Reed, PhD, is a nationally certified school psychologist who works at the elementary school level in Prince George's County Public Schools in Maryland. She graduated from Loyola University Chicago in 2020 and was the recipient of two university awards for her dissertation titled "Investigating Exclusionary Discipline: Teachers, Deficit Thinking, and Root Cause Analysis." Dr. Reed also received awards for her dissertation work through the Society for the Study of School Psychology (SSSP) and the American Educational Research Association (AERA).

Dr. Reed is passionate about advancing educational equity for historically minoritized students, disrupting the school-to-prison pipeline, and identifying and implementing alternatives to suspension. She has presented at the community, state, and national levels on school discipline disparities and alternative approaches to punitive practices. As a biracial yet White-presenting woman, she believes in using her privilege to make a difference in the lives of others. Follow her on Twitter @drkelsiereed and Instagram @dr.kelsiereed. She also runs a social justice advocacy Instagram page @sassy4socialjustice.

ACKNOWLEDGMENTS

WHILE THIS IS a book by Kelsie and Byron, it represents collective thinking for and by educators. Thank you, first and foremost, to those who gave their time and allowed us to interview them (in no particular order): Cory Cain, Brandon Gamble, Tim Runge, Ashley Tucker, Nikole Hollins-Sims, and William Blake. Thank you to those who provided input via social media and other electronic forms (in no particular order): Cyndy Alvarez, Alma Rosario, Danielle Christy, Krista Rice, Katie Ploss, Richard Williams, Shannon Williamson, Jahsha Tabron, Amela Mandzukic, Andrew Ench, Pamela Tucker, Wendy Turner, Patricia Zahregian, Kelly Vailancourt, Mel Reggie, Lisa Peterson, Alexandria Lock, Haley Biddanda, Amanda Austin Borosh, Ashley Adams, Mike Sullivan, Jordan Grande, Justina Yohannan, Debra Neufield, Alex Franks-Thomas, Jennifer Cooper, Autumn Stokes, and Joe Chay. And finally, thank you to our amazing OG book study participants who read our draft manuscript and met with us weekly to discuss its contents and offer feedback (in no particular order): Carrie Silkie, Wendy Turner, Kelly Ego-Osuala, Leah Carrington, Jaron Roberson, Sandra Green Hawkins, Karin Dykeman, Teryn Henderson, and Erika Wood. Every single person named here helped us immensely in pulling all our ideas together and ensuring that we centered the voices of those of us in the trenches!

Finally, we respectfully dedicate this book to the youth who march onward and upward.

BYRON'S PERSONAL ACKNOWLEDGMENTS

To my children, who are smart, brave, funny, and cool. Brayden, my oldest son. You are charismatic, a great dancer, inquisitive, insightful, analytical, and destined to change the world. Adelyn, you are the life of the party, a source of positive energy, a natural gymnast, and a jokester. You are always down to have an impromptu dance party with me and teach me to enjoy every moment. Brendan, my newborn son. You are the coolest baby in the world. I can tell you are content, curious, and already have a great sense of humor. Audria, my wife and mother of my children. You are the source of strength for our family. You are the strongest person I know. I love you and the children dearly. I respectfully dedicate this book to my wife Audria, and our children, Brayden, Addie, and Brendan—if it's up, then it's stuck—and we stuck.

To my parents, my dad, Bruce McClure, my beautiful mom, Bernice McClure, and my three big brothers, Marcus, Ed, and Brian, I love you all dearly. Ed, I look up to you because you are the strongest, most resilient person and have been an example for me, even when you might not know it. Thanks for teaching me what being strength-based means in action.

I also would like to thank my coauthor, Kelsie Reed. Without you, this book wouldn't exist. I'm grateful for the opportunity to have shared in this creation together. Working with you has been so much fun, and we complement each other perfectly. You are thoughtful, analytical, organized, and patient, and you can brilliantly reframe my wild ideas. I am honored and thankful to have written this book with you!

KELSIE'S PERSONAL ACKNOWLEDGMENTS

To my family and friends who have always supported my ambitious endeavors and everyone else I've crossed paths with from graduate school and up until today, thank you for the encouragement and for believing in me. Mom and Dad—you've always been my biggest cheerleaders, and I will forever appreciate the drive you instilled in me. Grandpa Ben and Grandma Jackie—I can't thank you both enough for letting me be your third roommate throughout the pandemic. You both have seen me at my best, worst, most confident, and most stressed from a virtual dissertation defense, a pandemic graduation, to my first big-girl job to the writing of this book. Thanks for loving and supporting me through it all. And finally—to all of my younger cousins, but especially to my littlest baby cousins, Zuri and Alimayu, y'all keep me going. I will forever fight for a world and system that lifts you up and shines nothing but the brightest light on your excellence.

Last but certainly not least, I also want to thank my coauthor, Byron McClure, for inviting me to join this endeavor with him. I would have never guessed that meeting you during my third year of graduate school at a national conference would lead to us coauthoring a book together five years down the road. I, too, agree that we complement each other tremendously! Your positivity, creativity, big picture thinking, and aspirations for success are just what this book needed to come together so authentically, meaningfully, energetically, and wholly.

NOTES

REFRAME 1

Gorski, Paul C. "Unlearning Deficit Ideology and the Scornful Gaze: Thoughts on Authenticating the Class Discourse in Education." *Teaching and Teacher Education* 25, no. 2 (February 2009): 309–18. https://doi.org/10.1016/j.tate.2008.07.008.

REFRAME 2

Durlak, Joseph A., Roger P. Weissberg, Allison B. Dymnicki, Rebecca D. Taylor, and Kriston B. Schellinger. "The Impact of Enhancing Students' Social and Emotional Learning: A Meta-Analysis of School-Based Universal Interventions." *Child Development* 82, no. 1 (January 2011): 405–32. https://doi.org/10.1111/j.1467-8624.2010.01564.x.

Hosp, John L., and Daniel J. Reschly. "Disproportionate Representation of Minority Students in Special Education: Academic, Demographic, and Economic Predictors." *Exceptional Children* 70, no. 2 (January 2004): 185–99. https://doi.org/10.1177/001440290407000204.

"Feature: Gorski." n.d. My.aasa.org. Accessed May 25, 2022. https://my.aasa.org/AASA/Resources/SAMag/May16/Gorski.aspx.

Love, Bayard, and Deena Hayes-Greene. "Diverse and Learner Ready Teachers (DLRT)." Accessed June 23, 2022. https://www.isbe.net/dlrt.

REFRAME 3

Boneshefski, Michael J., and Timothy J. Runge. "Addressing Disproportionate Discipline Practices Within a School-Wide Positive Behavioral Interventions and Supports Framework." *Journal of Positive Behavior Interventions* 16, no. 3 (2013): 149–158.

Davis, A. (2015). "How We Are Complicit: Challenging the School Discourse of Adolescent Reading." *Journal of Educational Controversy,* 9(1), 1–7.

Dudley-Marling, Curt, and Sarah Michaels (2012). "High-Expectation Curricula: Helping All Students Engage in Powerful Learning." *Teachers College Press.*

Preuss, Paul G. (2015). "School Leader's Guide to Root Cause Analysis." Routledge.

Myers, Lesli Clara, and Kara S. Finnigan. "Using Data to Guide Difficult Conversations around Structural Racism" (2018). *Annenberg Institute for School Reform.*

Reed, Kelsie (2020). "Investigating Exclusionary Discipline: Teachers, Deficit Thinking, and Root Cause Analysis." Dissertations (January). https://ecommons.luc.edu/luc_diss/3820/.

REFRAME 4

Guerra, P. L., & Z. C. Wubbena (2017). Teacher beliefs and classroom practices: Cognitive dissonance in high stakes and test-influenced environments. *Issues in Teacher Education.*

Guerra, P. L. & S. W. Nelson, (2010). Use a systematic approach for deconstructing and reframing deficit thinking. *Cultural Proficiency, 31*(2), 55–56.

Valencia, Richard R. (2010). *Dismantling Contemporary Deficit Thinking: Educational Thought and Practice.* Routledge.

Carter Andrews, D. J. & M. Gutwein, (2017). "Maybe that concept is still with us": Adolescents' racialized and classed perceptions of teachers' expectations. *Multicultural Perspectives, 19*(1), 5–15.

"Reframing Deficit Thinking: How to Change Perceptions for the Better." Free Spirit Publishing Blog. June 18, 2018. https://freespiritpublishingblog.com/2018/06/18/reframing-deficit-thinking-how-to-change-perceptions-for-the-better/.

Hambacher, E., and W. C. Thompson, (2015). Breaking the mold: Thinking beyond deficits. *Journal of Educational Controversy, 9*(1), 1–17.

Weiner, L. Challenging deficit thinking. *Educational Leadership, 64*(1), 42–45.

Seaton, F. S. (2018). Empowering teachers to implement a growth mindset. *Educational Psychology in Practice, 34*(1), 41–57.

"The Power of the Pygmalion Effect." n.d. Center for American Progress. https://www.americanprogress.org/article/the-power-of-the-pygmalion-effect/.

REFRAME 5

Seligman, M. E. P., T.A. Steen, N. Park, and C. Peterson (2005). Positive Psychology Progress: Empirical Validation of Interventions. *American Psychologist, 60*(5), 410–421. https://doi.org/10.1037/0003-066X.60.5.410.

REFRAME 6

"ACCUEIL." n.d. Apate. Accessed May 25, 2022. https://www.apate.fr.

Armstrong, Thomas, and Ebrary Inc. (2012). *Neurodiversity in the Classroom: Strength-Based Strategies to Help Students with Special Needs Succeed in School and Life.* ASCD.

Dudley-Marling, Curt. "The Resilience of Deficit Thinking." *Journal of Teaching and Learning* 10, no. 1, August 31, 2015. doi:10.22329/jtl. v10i1.4171.

Dudley-Marling, C., and M. B. Burns, (2018). Two perspectives on inclusion in the United States. *Global Education Review, 1*(1), 14–31.

Bilal, Rashad (2021). "The Financial Revolution" TEDxBuckhead. YouTube. https://www.youtube.com/watch?v=4-boHirZni8.

Smagorinsky, Peter, Joseph Jay Tobin, and Kyunghwa Lee (2019). "Dismantling the Disabling Environments of Education: Creating New Cultures and Contexts for Accommodating Difference." Peter Lang Publishing.

"The Deficit Model Is Harming Your Students." n.d. Edutopia. Accessed May 25, 2022. https://www.edutopia.org/blog/deficit-model-is-harming-students-janice-lombardi#:~:text=Raise%20your%20underserved%20students.

REFRAME 7

Safir, Shane, Jamila Dugan, Carrie Wilson, and Christopher Edmin (2021). *Street Data: A Next-Generation Model for Equity, Pedagogy, and School Transformation.* Corwin.

Jones, Kenneth, and Tema Okun (2001). "White Supremacy Culture from Dismantling Racism" https://www.thc.texas.gov/public/upload/preserve/museums/files/White_Supremacy_Culture.pdf.

Gallup, Inc. (2019). "Measure What Matters Most for Student Success." Gallup.com. https://www.gallup.com/education/233537/gallup-student-poll.aspx.

"About – Courageous Conversation" (2017). Courageousconversation.com. https://courageousconversation.com/about/.

Garcia, S. B. and P. L. Guerra, (2004). Deconstructing deficit thinking: Working with educators to create more equitable learning environments. *Education and Urban Society, 36*(2), 150–168.

Liou, D. D., T. E. J. Marsh, and R. Antrop-Gonzalez (2017). "Urban sanctuary schools for diverse populations: Examining curricular expectations and school effectiveness for student learning." *Equity & Excellence in Education, 50*(1), 68–83.

McKenzie, K. B. and J. J. Scheurich, (2004). "Equity traps: A useful construct for preparing principals to lead schools that are successful with racially diverse students." *Educational Administration Quarterly, 40,* 601–632.

Patton Davis, L., and S. D. Museus (2019). "What is deficit thinking? An analysis of conceptualizations of deficit thinking and implications for scholarly research."

REFRAME 8

Seligman, Martin (2018). "PERMA and the building blocks of well-being." *The Journal of Positive Psychology*, DOI: 10.1080/17439760.2018.1437466.

McGrath, R. E. (2017). "Technical Report: The VIA Assessment Suite for Adults: Development and Evaluation." VIA Institute on Character.

McGrath, R. E. (2019). Technical Report: The VIA Assessment Suite for Adults: Development and Initial Evaluation, Revised Edition." VIA Institute on Character.

Shoshani, A. (2019). "Young children's character strengths and emotional well-being: development of the Character Strengths Inventory for Early Childhood (CSI-EC)." *The Journal of Positive Psychology*, 14, 86–102. doi:10.1080/174 39760.2018.1424925.

Shoshani, A., and L. Shwartz (2018). From character strengths to children's well-being: Development and validation of the character strengths inventory for elementary school children. *Frontiers in Psychology*, 9, 2123. doi:10.3389/fpsyg.2018.02123/full.

MORE FROM
TIMES 10 PUBLICATIONS

Browse all titles at 10Publications.com

Hacking School Discipline

9 Ways to Create a Culture of Empathy & Responsibility Using Restorative Justice

By Nathan Maynard and Brad Weinstein

Reviewers proclaim this *Washington Post* Bestseller to be "maybe the most important book a teacher can read, a must for all educators, fabulous, a game changer!" Teachers and presenters Nathan Maynard and Brad Weinstein demonstrate how to eliminate punishment and build a culture of responsible students and independent learners in a book that will become your new blueprint for school discipline. Eighteen straight months at #1 on Amazon and still going strong, *Hacking School Discipline* is disrupting education like nothing we've seen in decades—maybe centuries.

Hacking Classroom Management

10 Ideas To Help You Become the Type of Teacher They Make Movies About

By Mike Roberts

Learn the ten ideas you can use today to create the classroom any great movie teacher would love. Utah English Teacher of the Year and sought-after speaker Mike Roberts brings you quick and easy classroom management Hacks that will make your classroom the place to be for all your students. He shows you how to create an amazing learning environment that makes discipline, rules, and consequences obsolete, no matter if you're a new teacher or a thirty-year veteran teacher.

Browse all titles at 10Publications.com

Hacking Student Learning Habits
9 Ways to Foster Resilient Learners and Assess the Process, Not the Outcome
By Elizabeth Jorgensen

Traditional outcome-based grades make school a place of right or wrong answers—a rigid system that impedes enjoyment and learning. In contrast, innovative teachers of all subjects and grade levels use process-based assessment to build positive classroom cultures and help students focus on the learning, not the grades. Award-winning writer and teacher Elizabeth Jorgensen shows how to create process-based assessments that help students develop habits of higher-order thinking. It is about embracing, trying, failing, and trying again. It is about turning "What did you get on the test?" into "How did you get that on the test?"

Quit Point
Understanding Apathy, Engagement, and Motivation in the Classroom
By Adam Chamberlin and Svetoslav Matejic

Authors Chamberlin and Matejic present a new way of approaching the Quit Point—their theory on how, why, and when people quit and how to stop quitting before it happens. Their insights will transform how teachers reach the potential of every student. *Quit Point* reveals how to confront apathy and build student engagement; how to differentiate learning for all levels; interventions to challenge students to keep going; and applications and toolkits to help you address the Quit Point, starting tomorrow.

Browse all titles at 10Publications.com

Hacking School Culture

Designing Compassionate Classrooms

By Angela Stockman and Ellen Feig Gray

Bullying prevention and character-building programs are deepening our awareness of how today's kids struggle and how we might help, but many agree: they aren't enough to create school cultures where students and staff flourish. This inspired Angela Stockman and Ellen Feig Gray to seek out systems and educators who were getting things right and share their findings in this insightful book.

Hacking Engagement

50 Tips & Tools to Engage Teachers and Learners Daily

By James Alan Sturtevant

If you're a teacher who appreciates quick ideas to engage your students, this is the book for you. *Hacking Engagement* provides fifty unique, exciting, and actionable tips and tools that you can apply right now. Try one of these amazing engagement strategies tomorrow: engage the enraged, create celebrity couple nicknames, hash out a hashtag, avoid the war on yoga pants, let your freak flag fly, become a proponent of the exponent, and transform your class into a focus group. Are you ready to engage?

Browse all titles at 10Publications.com

RESOURCES FROM TIMES 10 PUBLICATIONS

10Publications.com

Nurture your inner educator:

10Publications.com/educatortype

Podcasts:

hacklearningpodcast.com

jamesalansturtevant.com/podcast

On Twitter:

@10Publications

@HackMyLearning

#Times10News

#RealPBL

@LeadForward2

#LeadForward

#HackLearning

#HackingLeadership

#MakeWriting

#HackingQs

#HackingSchoolDiscipline

#LeadWithGrace

#QuietKidsCount

#ModernMentor

#AnxiousBook

#HackYourLibrary

All things Times 10:

10Publications.com

TIMES 10 PUBLICATIONS provides practical solutions that busy educators can read today and use tomorrow. We bring you content from experienced teachers and leaders, and we share it through books, podcasts, webinars, articles, events, and ongoing conversations on social media. Our books and materials help turn practice into action. Stay in touch with us at 10Publications.com and follow our updates on Twitter @10Publications and #Times10News.

Made in United States
Orlando, FL
22 November 2022

24889763R00137